Lessons
From The
Financial
Markets
For
2013

ZAK MIR

ADVFN BOOKS

CONTENTS

Introduction

My first book *101 Charts for Trading Success* was inspired by my former boss and "mentor" Tom Winnifrith, just after he cut my pay in the autumn of 2010. The book was completed by the end of December 2010 in terms of the writing although it took another couple months to tidy up and translate into a recognisable human language. I looked around for a publisher but was dismayed that I would not be able to get it published in paper form but as an ebook, something which I regarded as a rather inferior type of medium. This state of affairs has of course changed over the past couple of years and ebooks are now all the rage, although I would guess that most of us who are 40 and above still do not regard a book as being the real deal unless a tree has been involved.

It also seemed that ebooks have the problem of being rather cheaper than their paper equivalent and therefore it would seem to require millions of copies to be sold in order for there to be big money extracted from this particular activity. However, by the Christmas of 2011 when it appeared that the 42,000 words of the book may go to waste, I asked the opinion of Dominick Picarda at the Investors Chronicle. He rather helpfully reassured me that ebooks are in fact the way to go and also having read the draft of what I sent him, was of the opinion that the book could be a decent prospect. The story was completed when I saw an advert on the ADVFN.com looking for potential authors. They were not only happy to publish but also to sort the book out into a professional looking tome. They were also keen to entertain the prospect of publishing more books in future, which brings the story up to date.

Writing books seems to me about as easy as pulling teeth, especially when you have four young children under six, and even if you don't care about the financial aspect – where I am now. But as a compensation, the reality still seems to be that writing a book/being an author is an occupation that still punches well above its weight in terms of kudos, credibility and a general feel good factor when it goes well, far more than many other more difficult endeavours. That said, I would prefer being a rock star, even at the age of 46.

Therefore with this in mind I offer you *Lessons From The Financial Markets For 2013*. As much as anything else, I would suggest that the catalyst behind *Lessons*, was not the aforementioned Mr Winnifrith's fiscal frugality, but childhood memories of reading the *Guinness Book of World Records*. This book was and is of course a great inspiration to everyone in terms of humanity stretching themselves to the limit in all fields, and for a kid in the 70s when I was still hoping to be the next Winston Churchill, picking up the latest edition was always something of a treat. While *Lessons From The Markets* may not carry quite the same sense of wonder for all of its readers, I would hope that in future years its publication could be an annual event in terms of summing up the financial markets – one of the greatest melodramas the world has ever known – on an annual basis. In particular I would hope that it might spark interest in the younger generations to get involved in the financial markets, which – whatever the frequent scandals might imply – have been a pathway to successful non-rip-off careers for many, even those from the most humble of backgrounds.

Perhaps what should be noted as well is that while I am best known as a chartist, many of the lessons are non-charting lessons and more of psychological, emotional, lessons in life, as much as an illustration of how the markets work, and how general trading ideas can be derived.

A final point, and something which is of course worth bearing in mind, is that while we have a December publication date, obviously I have not been writing everything right at the end of 2012. Also I have not been able to include perhaps every single worthy stock or event in the financial area. The preparation and the writing of this book started from the beginning of October and therefore some guesses, and some predictions have been made in terms of what may be relevant by the end of the year and also where certain stocks and markets may go over that final part of 2012. Clearly, given that I am in the prediction game as a chartist, you would not expect this to be too much of a challenge, even though in some cases it may be slightly foolhardy to attempt to make a call on these particular situations. The fate of the Direct Line insurance float, or even whether Facebook might head for $0 by 31 December 2012, are a couple of challenges that come to mind.

This book is by its very nature a subjective exercise, and of course the contents are also skewed towards what may be most interesting after the event, even more so than while it is actually going on. For instance, while Hurricane Sandy was important enough and painful enough an event to close the New York Stock Exchange for the first time since 9/11, the price action/trading implications were relatively limited, and to put it bluntly, did not provide much to learn from in my opinion.

The financial markets are of course a massive area to look at, even in terms of the highlights over the past year. But I would be proud if I could convey at least some of the excitement, suspense, emotional swings, manias and gloom over past twelve months even while acknowledging that the best that can be done here is only to skim the surface. I suppose it is the way that they are skimmed which provides the interest.

2012 Perspectives:
The Overview

It would have been perfectively possible to have written this part of the book, Perspectives, just as easily and perhaps more logically at the end. But instead I have decided to have a summary/review of the past year at this stage in the proceedings. This is because I think that it's well worth looking at the key stocks, markets, and events, within the context of recent years as well as with a nod to the prevailing mood among those who are trading/investing. For instance, we are near the end of 2012 and so far it will be another year when the single currency, the Euro, remained in place as the single European currency, rather than losing one more of its weaker members such as Greece, or its patron Germany.

Given the way that it is rather difficult on this side of the English Channel to find anyone who is sympathetic to the cause of the EU, it may be worth noting that at least to this date the source of one of the world's greatest gravy trains outside the NHS is still very much alive and kicking. Indeed, with the appropriate amount of can kicking down the road it is difficult to see how the status quo may be changed at all unless we actually see war erupt between the constituent nations, or within them, the prevention of which of course was one of the main reasons why the EU was set up in the first place. I may be one of those who wish that this single European vision was one that was never created in the first place (Hitler tried and failed) now that it is with us, but some credit should be given to the concept as being a safety net for the weaker nations in times of economic difficulty. This is a role I believe that few can argue with. I shudder to think what would have happened to the likes of Greece, Spain and Italy in the wake of the sub-prime mortgage meltdown if there had been no EU to stabilise the situation, deliver bailouts and generally play for time. As far as the EU haters in the UK are concerned my message is, as follows: one of the main reasons it has not lived up to expectations is because the UK did not play a leading role in it from the start. Therefore it became the France/Germany versus the rest entity we are seeing it become now as one of the worst economic periods in history continues to bite. Indeed, that reminds me that if there has been any plus point from the disastrous 1930s style depression of the past few years, it is that only this once-a-century event was enough to reveal the flaws in the European ideal/set up, and therefore on that basis we should not judge it too harshly.

In mentioning the sub-prime mortgage meltdown, you can see where I lay the blame for much of the Europe's woes as I think that the flaws in the EU set up might never have been revealed – no Eurobond was a laughable omission. In fact, it should have been no single currency without any Eurobond, and if not the EU should have simply remained a free trade area. Perhaps on this basis it was both ironic and encouraging that one of the big plus points on a fundamental basis from 2012 was the beginning of a recovery in the US housing market. In a strange and equally wonderful way in the early autumn of this year as well, both the Dow and the S&P managed to beat their Credit Crunch highs, effectively shaking off the misery of the past five years Stateside. No doubt, there was great joy across the pond for all but the Republican party, whose Presidential contender Mitt Romney was the unfortunate victim, especially from the perspective of someone trying to win four years in the White House. In the end he lost because he didn't have the appeal with women voters (all those binders)/was too rich, too old (politicians are increasingly forty-something when in their prime), and apart from a talent for putting his foot in his mouth like his father, he was also evidently unlucky – a real vote loser. At least he isn't bald . . . He really should have stood down during the campaign, yes, he was that cringe-worthy at times, and I am no Democrat.

Unfortunately, the bulk of the economic newsflow was improving over the year going into the 6 November election – a nod to the bad luck Romney had. Perhaps the final kick in the teeth for his campaign came with the early September QE3 announcement from the Federal Reserve, something which broke the unwritten rule not to deliver any action that may throw the result of the key US vote. Of course, the Fed and the country was probably more concerned as to whether the Fiscal Cliff could be avoided, rather than whether Gaffe Meister Romney was given a level playing field with which to fight No Drama Obama (and no action apart from ending Bin Laden's retirement). Indeed, it was rather fortunate that the latest Israel/Hamas rocket firing festival only escalated on the right side of the US election not to render Mr Obama's pre-emptive Nobel Peace Prize as being as much of the kiss of death that its latest award of this bauble is likely to be for the EU over the next few years.

Here in the UK there was not the same degree of tumultuous activity as seen in either the EU or the US, but more a continuation of the Public School sixth former Coalition Government, with its added twist of Dad's Army as supplied by business Secretary Vince Cable. Of course there were the high moments such as the Diamond Jubilee and the Olympics, which were used by failing companies as an excuse for losing money, and by successful companies as the reason that they were doing better than ever. We flipped from a narrow double-dip recession, one that had been on the cards for at least a couple of years, to the joy and elation of emerging from this dismal state of affairs in Q3. In some ways the real standouts over here were actually what didn't change. Amongst the most important were perhaps the UK's triple-A rating which means that it can finance its double PIIGS nation sized deficit at a fraction of the cost on the basis of nothing else other than being a semi-detached member of the EU. Presumably, if this AAA status does go we would see a wobble in the stock market and for economic prospects, but it is still the case that the City of London's propped upright safe haven status is probably keeping enough freshly laundered, non tax paid cash coming in to our green and pleasant land to withstand all but the worst of macro economic disasters. This should include the prospect of the US going over the edge of a Fiscal Cliff in 2013, especially as once again our safe haven status would be underpinned and in many instances enhanced. So, overall, the lesson for us in Blighty in 2012 is that it pays not to be European or American. The problem for 2013 and beyond is, for how long we can manage to pull off this double negative equals positive winning strategy?

Much may depend on one key area, the banking sector. Over the past five years this area of our economy has proved to be a combination of our Achilles Heel and the goose that lays the golden egg. That said, given the way that they don't pay much tax, don't lend, don't do as they are told, and as far as RBS (RBS) and Lloyds Banking (LLOY) are concerned have cost us £66bn that we will probably never see again, it is quite difficult to work out which part of the golden goose is actually golden? Feel free to email Chancellor George Osborne as apparently he has the answer and was pontificating as such in November. It is a bit like having Amazon (AMZN) and Starbucks (SBUX) in the UK, great for getting people off the street and out of trouble, but as they pay next to no tax, of little use other than flattening the unemployment rate.

Of course, 2012 marked five years into the economic crisis, and as I have seen from his flash ads on Sky News, young Ed Conway has identified that Western Economies may be rushing headlong into the Japanese Model of rolling stagnation. This was almost guaranteed from the day that quantitative easing was introduced in the wake of the 2007 credit crunch, and the day that interest rates were lowered, instead of being increased as they have been on every single other slump since the Second World War. Apparently after nearly 22 years the Japanese are on QE9, while after five years we are on QE3 as far as the US is concerned. In fact, for them QE was a failed strategy that they started in the late 90s and gave up just a few years later. Just why we revived this particular dead duck remains something of a Keynsian whodunit. Even worse, we are already out of ammo in the sense that both the US and the EU have committed themselves to an unlimited magnitude of money printing for an unlimited period – a recognition that the strategy has not worked and that there is nothing else of substance to throw on the dying embers of the bonfire.

On this basis alone any bear worth their salt would have been mega short of the stock market from the middle of September when we had our last big tranche of concerted central bank intervention. Perhaps it is lucky that the stock market doesn't follow logic even at the best of times, and even with the most compelling reasons.

Indeed, the five-year anniversary of the credit crunch led to plenty of head-scratching amongst experts, gurus and assorted commentators, many of which thanks to the social media are of the armchair variety. There have been plenty of books released of the head-scratching variety, essentially asking the question, where did it all go wrong? I am dying to read them AFTER I have finished this book. One would be Robert Peston's *How Do We Fix This Mess?* The other is Roger Bootle's *The Trouble with Markets: Saving Capitalism From Itself.* That said, there are two problems with both of these books, however well they make their point – it is that the one thing you can guarantee is that they will have no influence whatever on those in a position to affect economic policy. Perhaps this is related to the way that both Peston and Bootle are too much establishment figures in their own right to carry any sting in what they write, but not close enough to those with economic power to act as a force for change. In addition, as far as fixing the mess that we are in, the mistake five years ago was attempting to fix the crisis. Capitalism means cycles of boom and bust, and the more you try to intervene, the worse the bust becomes. The problem is that since Japan's bust in the 1990s we have in the West found bust unacceptable, hence all the QE.

Of course, the other highlight of the past five years is the way that as well as the credit crunch crisis in developed countries making them go bust, emerging markets have sucked their money away, and the baby boomer demographic time bomb went off too. This means that over the past decade we have fallen off a demographic cliff with not enough money to go around, especially with relation to the level of post-war welfare we're accustomed to. I could go on but the Peston/Bootle/Nial Ferguson/what a clever boy I am approach doesn't really do it for me at the moment.

Perspectives 2012:
A More Personal View

It is now over a decade since I first started appearing on CNBC and Bloomberg as a technical analyst/strategist, both for my website Zaks-TA.com, and assorted brokerages. There was a certain novelty in being a non-aligned, independent commentator spouting the latest charting angle in an area which had been previously dominated by the big City institutions and their stuffy/snooty attitudes. Their representatives always appeared claiming to be facing the right direction as far as the markets were concerned at any given time. Of course, hardly any of these big names have survived the past decade in the same form that they were in back then, and many have lost billions via their unfortunate patsies such as Kweko Adoboli at UBS, calling the market wrong in a way that even rookie traders would have struggled to do. But for some reason, you can still tune into financial TV and see these apparently omniscient and infallible gods continue to propagate their self-aggrandizing market myths. By the way, who is going to fine the FSA for yet another being-asleep-at-the-wheel job in terms of UBS?

Incidentally, I went back to CNBC and Bloomberg this year for the first time in six years to find the landscape quite changed. If nothing else, technical analysis is no longer the tea leaf reading horoscope style babble that it was regarded as even as recently as ten years ago – it appears to be a hot subject. On this occasion I went back as senior analyst at the Institute of Trading and Portfolio Management, a company set up by former Goldman Sachs and JPMorgan Chase trader Anton Kreil. He is set to be the first man to trade from space in 2014, something which the aged schoolboy that I am can only admire. But even more I'm looking forward to the Institute being my final destination in terms of being the appropriate place for my particular skill set. It is a community of high net worth, expert, educated traders, who so far have taught me rather more than I have taught them. The learning process continues.

The Winner's Podium 2012

1. Apple: The First Year After Steve Jobs

The Set Up

Perhaps like most people I would like to pride myself on being an original. This means that all things being equal I occasionally think of the original perspective that nobody else has on a topical debate, spot a flaw in an argument which has been taken for granted as a winning one, or find an angle on an issue which is unique – and hopefully better than anything else on the table at that point. Unfortunately, this is increasingly a more and more difficult thing to do in the age of the Internet. Now there are billions of bloggers with attendant opinions and ideas, and you would have thought that on every issue including Apple, one of the most talked about phenomena of the past ten years, not one stone would remain unturned in terms of the views on the world's largest company.

Therefore I also apologise if what I am going to say is not an original point and is something which every blogger in town has already pointed out. Nevertheless, I believe the following unusual form of analysis still stands. It was interesting that on 5 October 2012, which was a year after the death of Steve Jobs, we actually saw a technical signal combining with the anniversary of his death. What is even more curious is the way that this break of 12 September support at $656 in the first week of October tied in almost exactly with the end of the average length of grief which is said to be one year. If you look up the Banned Blogger's article on ADVFN.com "Apple: Rotten To The Core" you will see the call I made at the time on the shares being a sell.

Indeed, if you believe in the comments on www.caring.com, that it takes about a year for someone to feel better (return to normal) after the death of a loved one, then you may agree that this concept could be one that would affect not only sentiment towards Apple, but also the share price. Of course, turning the argument around in terms of how Apple would do in terms of the price action, this would mean that for the first year after Steve Jobs' passing the stock was in something of period of grace where nobody would really feel like knocking it down in a serious way. This is even after a fiasco such as the mapping app and the general situation where the company is involved in ugly vanity legal battles with Samsung. That said, the most pertinent factor of all may be that new CEO could never live up to the legend that his predecessor had built up. On this basis I would suggest that Apple mania had an extra year more than it deserved courtesy of the late Mr Jobs passing. It is now five years since the iPhone was launched in June 2007, and for any mania – including that of the Beatles 1963-1966 (until the Beatles said they were greater than Jesus), Tulips in Holland (1634-7) and the Dotcom Bubble of 1995-2001, this has to be regarded as a long time. To paraphrase Winston Churchill's speech of 10 November 1942, we may have reached the end of the beginning of Apple's great bull run. Are Apple products so good looking you want to eat them? Yes. Are they the perfect affordable luxury for straightened times? Yes. Should Apple be the world's most valuable company? Maybe, but probably not.

2012 Price Action

The daily chart of Apple overlaps into the end of 2011 on the basis that the end of November witnessed a rebound for the stock of the then rising black 200 day moving average at $363. This is important as it is usually the case that some of the strongest rallies in stocks and markets are derived from a successful pullback to the 200 day line, and to a lesser extent the shorter timeframe 10, 20 and 50 day lines. In fact the big action for 2012 started almost at the open in the form of a gap in the first training session of the year through towards $410, with a larger feature the gap through $440 towards the end of the month, both of which remained unfilled. It is normally the case of when you see two unfilled gaps in relatively quick succession the correct assumption is that we are heading for a significant move to the upside.

Indeed, if we needed any further proof of the resilience of the Apple price action it was the February gap through $480. From this moment on one would be merely choosing which moving average to use as a trailing stop loss, in this case the grey 20 day moving average and only reversing or taking profits on long positions if there was a sustained push below the 20 day line. The best trigger in such instances is normally to use an end of day close below the moving average which is being used as the dynamic stop loss. As can be seen there was no end of day close below the 20 day line until 13 April and a $603 close. On the basis of the break of a December RSI trendline the end of the first phase of Apple's 2012 rally came on 30

March, $599, a little early as far as the 10 April peak of $644. After that traders were left in the lurch for just a few weeks in terms of waiting on a big signal from Apple shares. 23 April $556 intraday low resentfully as after a break at the level down to $528 we were waiting on any end of day close back above the former April low to suggest a bear trap and a new potential led to the upside. This was delivered on 21 May in the form of end of day close at $561. Those who kept their nerve could have stayed in the stock from there until the $700 plus all-time high, although the final buy signal of note in terms of people argument came on 31 July. Here we would have bought in on the basis of a three-day island bottom being formed, with its $603 open price of that day the notional entry-level.

Then for August/September/October we have a clear head and shoulders reversal pattern, one that is backed by a beautiful island top sell formation just above the $700 mark. The presence of this island top, as well as the head and shoulders reversal, reminds us that so-called double or combination signals have to be taken as a compelling event in terms of trading action. Indeed, on this occasion we had a break of a May RSI support line around the 46 level coinciding with the aforementioned one-year death anniversary for Steve Jobs, and the reversal signals in the price window. From that point on a fill of the $585 late July gap up floor became the objective for the iPhone maker's stock. In fact, this objective was easily beaten by the beginning of November, arguably causing the biggest private investor upset of the year as their beloved Apple tanked despite iPhone 5 and the Mini iPad launches.

Payoff

Of course, there could easily be a whole book describing Apple's year every year, and particularly the one after the death of Steve Jobs. Standouts have been the record high as far as the stock is concerned, the most expensive company in the world tag, the maps app fiasco, and on-going legal warfare with Samsung. The suspicion here at the beginning of October when I first started writing about Apple's year was that we may have seen at least a pause in the progress for the iPhone maker was partly psychological – the one year after Jobs, partly to do with the daily chart, where there was a clear double reversal/triple reversal. This proved to be correct and was more than just yet another attempt to be a contrarian who managed to pin the correct price target tail on the world's largest donkey (company). Before the fall one could only imagine how much money has been lost by speculators in previous months attempting to short this stock and of course from October it was the longs who took a massive hit. Clearly it would always be best to miss out on such money-losing opportunities in both directions, and from my perspective following technical signals is one of a few robust methods of doing this if you decouple your personal psychology from what your eyes are telling you on the screen. Incidentally, by the end of November for Apple the unfilled gap to the upside on 19 November completed that month's island bottom reversal, with the entry point the open of 20 November at just under $572. That said, we really need to witness an end of day close back above the November gap at $580 to suggest that it is not merely a dead cat bounce the stock is offering.

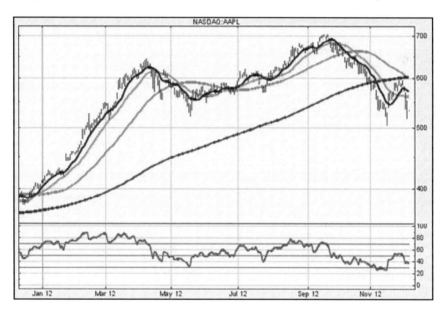

2. Facebook: Faking It

The Set Up

IPOs are one of the most serious/pivotal business days as far as any company is concerned, very often the all-time highlight. To my mind the IPO day is on a par with the wedding day as far as a marriage is concerned. That is to say in the near-term and possibly even on a longer timeframe almost whatever happens the day of the IPO will be a high point. In other more cynical terms it could be said that it is downhill from there. Perhaps the timing of Zuckerberg's wedding was an acknowledgement of this? This means that even if the company in question does go on to create massive profits and does fantastically well, the chance of making money from the share price directly from the IPO price initially is very rare.

There is also another lesson in terms of the run-up to IPOs, especially the major ones such as Facebook or the UK Direct Line (DLG) this year. It is that in general whatever the state of the market is at the time the grey market is being formulated, there is stone, cold silence regarding the pitfalls and uncertainties surrounding the prospects of the company in question. Instead, you get emails from stockbrokers and their introducers urging you to take part in this wonderful opportunity as if it was for a Christmas raffle in which every ticket is a winner.

Magically, no one takes notice of killjoys like myself until all the money is in the kitty. I disagreed with Direct Line being floated on the basis that we the public already own 82% of it, as it belongs to part-nationalised RBS. This 82% of course is not a killer blow, but there is a principle at stake!

My general rule is therefore unless there is an obvious buy signal for a stock soon after it comes to market, you should normally wait a few months until a couple of trading updates have come through and the puff and bluster of the prospectus has been blown away. This is because of the problem of relatively few siren voices getting an airing before the IPO, and then normally too many cynics being unleashed after the float date.

But at least out of the wreckage of the first few days of Facebook, my friend and financial markets guru Alpesh Patel did manage to get recorded on the BBC in May saying that the shares would half, and they promptly did by September. The question of course was what to do after they had halved in value? According to conventional valuations – and I would take the word of my "mentor" Tom Winnifrith on this subject – on the basis of conventional earnings per share or the price earnings ratio and a general back of the envelope assessment, the real value of Facebook should probably be no more than five dollars a share.

I have to admit that although Facebook may be a little too friendly for my personality style, I am a fan and feel rather bruised at such a low valuation. Indeed, during the year I did write about my personal way of valuing new economy stocks. This is based on the experience of the dot-com bubble and what it taught us, as well as a knowledge that the Internet of the early 2000s is very similar to the railroads of the 19th century and companies that formed around that, as well as of course the first oil companies and the first car manufacturers in the last century.

It can be said quite simply on the basis of railroad, oil/cars, dot-com, that being first in any field should command a premium. If there is a bubble once again in the new economy it is because we are realising that many of the big names that have now become household names such as eBay (EBAY), Amazon (AMZN), and Facebook are companies that have a massive and probably permanent advantage. It is well known that in the old economy larger companies will take over their smaller rivals just in order to knock out the competition and thereby increase their growth and earnings prospects. In the case of the new economy, Facebook was the first major social media player and should be valued not in terms of how much its revenues or turnover is, but how much it would cost another company to create a new entity with similar market share. The best example of my argument comes from the Microsoft takeover of Skype in 2011 for $8.5 billion, a valuation that represented 32 times earnings. Commentators scoffed at the takeover, but my view is that it was a fair deal. If Microsoft wanted to replicate the Skype business and have as many users while Skype was still in business, it would not have been able to do this for $8.5bn or even $80bn. Coincidentally, 32 p/e is what Facebook's will fall to in 2013 according to Business Insider. I have a feeling that the fate of Skype is what the fate of Facebook will be, if it gets cheap enough – $10-$15 – and perhaps even if it does not.

2012 Price Action

I suppose given how grossly overvalued Facebook shares are supposed to be according to the fundamental experts, who were curiously silent before the shares hit the stock market on 18 May, we should be grateful that even as much as one day was spent by the stock above its issue price. In fact the gap down the day after the IPO remains unfilled as do those of 16 and 27

July 16. Indeed, here we are in the inverse position to that of Apple described above pre-October, in that Facebook is showing us how consecutive gaps to the downside can deliver ultra-painful selloffs.

Bullish divergence in the RSI window gave us a rally from the start of September, with the gap higher through the grey 20 day moving average on 12 September particularly encouraging as it was forming an island bottom. Unfortunately the only thing which trumps an island bottom is an island top, one which came through on 24 September by a gap to the downside whose top is at $20.60. In fact the whole problem of the price action for Facebook between September and November 2012 is that it was essentially just a collection of alternating island tops and bottoms with an overall $19-$24 range.

Going into the final quarter of 2012 Facebook needed to deliver at least an end of day close back above the July gap down at $26.73 in order to begin to be a serious contender as a bottom fishing opportunity. As things stand it would appear to be something of a thankless task in trying to find the suitable entry point for the long-term unless, or until, this is achieved. But even though the task was thankless I did start to attempt in October to look for the conditions which might lead to the shares staging a turnaround. For some reason I had it in my mind that the decline from the opening day will eventually be reversed in the form of a U-shaped turnaround. In fact, the suspicion was that the 14 November end of day close back above the top of an October gap at $21.88 may have been the beginning of the end of the bear run for Facebook. By the end of November we were looking for sustained price action above the floor of the July gap at $24.54 to cement the nascent recovery idea. While of course the sensible thing would probably be to wait for $26.73 as described above, at least just before the time of publication the social media stock was making very interesting technical noises indeed. It really would not be surprising if that little three-day dip of the start of September below $18.50 was the selling climax point here. Put it this way, during the early autumn I did predict that Facebook could hit $45 during early 2013, and so far there is nothing which has happened which makes this appear less likely.

Payoff

Following on from the rather grandiose technical prediction, it will be intriguing to see whether the doomsters are really proved to be correct regarding the overvaluation of the social media group, and of course how foolish so many people were in buying at the IPO. While they may be correct in theory, and even in practice, on this occasion I would prefer to take the bull tack just so that the I told you so brigade are left reeling.

3. Google (GOOG): Fat Finger

The Set Up

Basically my favourite US stocks are that tech giant trio of Facebook, Apple and Google, and a chart that I examine at any excuse, even when there is no real reason to do so. The explanation is that I am fascinated by this area of the stock market both on a technical and fundamental basis, especially given the way that as a kid in the 1970s I believed that we would have reached our current level of technological sophistication in the 1990s not the 2010s. While these companies are undoubtedly great in terms of each being ahead of the curve in their own particular way, somehow in the 1970s and 1980s technology just bided its time.

But moving on to search engine Google, I was actually wondering before starting on *Lessons From The Financial Markets*, whether apart from the charting aspect there would be enough to talk about as far as Google is concerned in terms of newsflow. Luckily, the incredible fat finger episode of 18 October when there was an 11% plunge in the share price due to a prematurely released 20% profits dive announcement means that Google is a worthy topic as one of the stocks of the year.

2012 Price Action

The reason that Google may be great as far as the technical aspect of being part of *Lessons* is that the year started off nearly as badly as it ended in terms of the price action of the shares. This is because there was a 9% share price decline and associated gap down at the end of January on a revenue targets miss. However, it may have been at that time the share price was helped along by a generally very positive stock market as a whole, and the gap down through the 50 day moving average with a stock or rebounding above both the $560 level and the 200 day moving average – effectively a buy signal. But it can be said that from the second half of the year is when the real fireworks started in terms of the price action at Google. June-July saw bullish divergence in the RSI window and a narrow bear trap below the $564 January floor, with the worst level in June being $557. Ironically, it was a 19 July gap through the 50 day moving average to the upside which ended the bear phase started off in January with the opposite move to the downside. What helps here is that the move to the upside was so extended that even the traditionally late 50 day 200 day moving average golden cross buy signal at the end of August had at least another $70 of upside for those who followed it. Perhaps what was the biggest day of the year technically for Google came in the form of a somewhat mysterious 8 October gap to the downside after a bull trap in the stock through $770 the Friday before.

This sell signal was certainly not obscure enough to have been missed by Google watchers, with the only spoiler being that one would probably never have imagined that such a relatively innocuous sell trigger could have led to such a big move to the downside. Of course, it is the narrowest and most marginal signals that very often deliver the biggest moves.

Payoff

Getting stuffed on Apple after all the hype of the new gadgets is one thing, but you would rather think of Google as a more robust fundamental prospect, and not for the herd who follow the big names in a kneejerk fashion. However, we were reminded with the Google fat finger episode that even the best companies can be vulnerable to so called Black Swan events of a surprisingly trivial aspect – the printer RR Donelley releasing the Q3 earnings report too early. In fact, it is likely that even without the botched release shares of Google would have taken a hit this autumn as the early October bull trap gap down was an evil looking technical sell signal. Fundamentally, the question is whether the general migration away from the desktop and onto mobile platforms is one which is somehow threatening the business model of the tech giant? It may also be the case that the competition is finally starting to catch up with a company that seemed to be always running five years into the future.

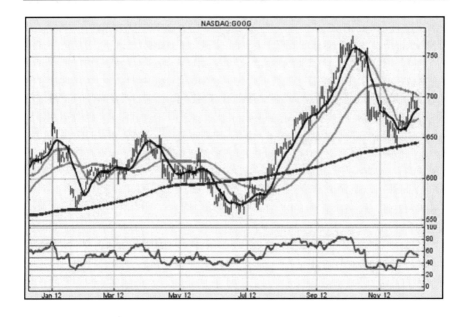

4. The Euro: Mission Irreversible

The Set Up

Perhaps the first thing to be said about the Euro is that for many commentators even being able to write about its price action over the past 12 months can be regarded as something of an achievement given the way that according to the Europhobes the single currency would/should have broken up in 2012, 2011, even 2010. But it is still here, and with it the dream of closer European integration in all its forms is just about being kept alive. Ironically, it would appear that due to the way that the common currency was set up, the lack of the Eurobond/properly coordinated economic policy, we are probably looking for gradually more intimate relationships between our continental cousins, arguable even more close than would have happened if the good old days before the credit crunch collapse in 2007 had continued.

A pet theory of mine (currently a minority of one theory) is that the credit crunch itself was a product of the Euro threatening to become the new world reserve currency, redirecting funds that would normally have supported US assets such as T bonds and US equities, and hence towards the latter part of the last decade led to the crunch that the United States exported around the developed world. Clearly, this is never likely to be a popular theory, especially in the US. That said, even if you buy the idea that the Euro was a victim of its own success, it seems like total madness to have launched the common currency without a common bond. But apparently the Germans prefer periodic cash handouts to southern European members and next to nothing on their Bunds rather than paying a little bit more than next to nothing on a Eurobond.

In this my belief is that they are incorrect in the sense that without the speculative shooting gallery of Italian, Greek, Spanish, Portuguese, and Irish bonds, a common European bond could have a proportionately cheaper rate than just the average of the individual members as they stand. Once again though, I admit that given the way the Germans/the ECB/the IMF managed to muddle through so long in avoiding what could be the ultimate cure for this disaster area, it really does seem that it is not going to happen. Indeed, money printing down to wheelbarrows sized wallets, or even debt forgiveness as was practised in ancient Rome at this time in the cycle, would appear to be more likely than a common bond.

But it was not all gloom and doom for the Euro in 2012. From July we were treated to the spectacle of a new hero for the financial markets – super Mario. Apparently in the cunning disguise of being just an ECB President, in Mario Draghi we were presented with someone with the foreign exchange trading skills of a George Soros combined with the poker playing talents of Stu Ungar (presumably without the attendant lifestyle.)

2012 Price Action

While it may have been the case in Back To The Future that 12 November 1955 was a date that had special significance in terms of being the temporal junction point of the entire space-time continuum, then 2 August 2012 became a key date for followers of the Euro. Perhaps it could be explained by saying that this was the day that King Canute, otherwise known as Mario Draghi, actually managed to turn the tide for the single currency. The low of that day was $1.2134, as compared to around $1.22 when he was giving his early afternoon press conference. And I have to say it was an incredible moment to be an observer of the financial markets. This is partly because when the ECB President said don't be short of the Euro the message to me was that even if this wasn't yet the low zone for the Euro, at last we had someone who would might be able to pull this advice off.

The price channel price action of the day said everything about a floor being put in for Euro/dollar. Of course, but anyone familiar with a recent history of equivalent positions where politicians/bankers/anyone in authority threw down the gauntlet/challenged the financial markets, they would normally end up with egg on their face for a lifelong period. Taking a random example, Chancellor Norman Lamont's green shoots of economic recovery in the early 90s in the aftermath of the ERM exit was an unsuccessful prototype of trying to talk up a situation which was essentially hopeless. But perhaps due to Draghi's technocrat credentials – a PhD from MIT helps, in this man we are talking of one of the winners in *Lessons*.

Looking at the daily chart of Euro/dollar from a broader brush perspective in terms of timeframe than on just one fateful day, we can see how a late October 2011 bull trap through the 200 day moving average, then still over $1.40, influenced the bulk of the first half of the year. Indeed from a technical point of view it can be said that the Draghi intervention at the end of July/beginning of August was all the more remarkable given the way that from the beginning of the year until that point we were seeing a steady progression to the downside with former support coming in as new resistance, and with very little overlap. Such price action normally ends with an acceleration to the downside, even by gaps, before it comes to an end. Instead what we saw here was what could be described as a near exhaustion gap to end the move to the downside on 20 and 23 July, helped by the way the price action of the two days just overlapped. The support line drawn through July and early August on the daily chart refers to the left- and right-hand shoulders of an inverted head and shoulders formation. At the time the most obvious buy signal multiple end of day close on 23 August back above the late June intraday low of $1.2407. This has the benefit of being consistently above the 50 day moving average as well as breaking initial August neckline resistance at $1.2443.

As far as the autumn's progress can be said, things actually got better and better technically as far as Euro/Dollar was concerned, the obvious breakthrough being a break above the 200 day moving average – something suggesting trend change to the upside during early September as QE3 fever was at its height. It can be seen how the October and September probes for support at the 200 day moving average involved just brief intraday touches by the price action. The overall effect was therefore very positive given that the support was well above previously comparable old June resistance below $1.2760. Given the major and very liquid market, such a difference between old support and new resistance is almost unheard of. Therefore, even as early as mid-October the expectation was that this was a cross that would take out its initial 2012 resistance well before the end of the year. While the November bear trap dip below the 200 day line eventually rendered such an idea too optimistic, the fact that the cross managed to flip back above a falling 200 day line was constructive enough to hint that the year could at least end with a reasonable low $1.30s flourish.

Payoff

While it may be the case that the US and its Fiscal Cliff eventually trump what has been happening in the Eurozone over the recent past, so far the Supreme Fudge Award goes to the EU in managing to delay the "inevitable" Eurozone breakup which my Eurosceptic/hating friends have been calling for the best part of three years as imminent, and which despite all the scares has so far not materialised. This is an example of what is obvious simply not happening, more obvious indeed than the asset bubble bursting in 2007-8, While 2013 may be the year, this issue of the Euro's demise has gone on so long now that at the very least it is likely not to be the apocalyptic event previously billed if only in shock value.

UK Banks

Barclays: The Ultimate Diamond Geezer

The Set Up

I have to admit that in terms of me and my memory, to suggest that it is like a sieve would be flattery. Nevertheless, what sticks out in my mind about *101 Charts*, now nearly two years old, is the way that the coverage of Barclays Bank was very much focused on the then head of its investment bank Barclays Capital. My description of Mr Diamond was as someone you would not want to meet in a dark alley, or indeed, any alley. In fact, he'd already been collecting comments in a similar vein, before his appointment as CEO of Barclays at the beginning of January 2011. What we now know, as was revealed in 2012, is that the FSA also felt that he may not be quite the perfect candidate as CEO. Like me they did nothing about it. I have the excuse that I was busy with other more pressing matters such as the writing on my website; presumably they were affected by contingencies of a similar nature. Another incentive these days not to nip a scandal in the bud is that there is no "result" to justify the existence of the regulator, and no £300m fine.

But it was interesting that this year I did run into someone who alleged to be a former employee of the FSA. He described the regulator as being an entity which is essentially the stepping stone for those wishing to get proper jobs in the city. On this basis their day-to-day "regulating" of firms such as Barclays and other financial groups is essentially a networking process ahead of them being given jobs around the City of London. Therefore, one would imagine that while FSA employees will always be keen to give the impression of being fully capable in what they are doing, the concept of not wanting to bite the hand that feeds them or may feed them in the future might come into play.

The idea also ties in with the concept that the only financial punishments we have seen have been limited ones in the form of fines rather than anything more serious such as closing down the relevant businesses or parts of businesses. Bank of Credit and Commerce International (BCCI) was closed 20 years ago on the basis largely I presume that it was founded by a Pakistani (my heritage), and secondly that massive money laundering was alleged. Massive money laundering at Standard Chartered (STAN) et al led only to fines. I see closing down a bank, if only as an example to others, as the only thing which would be a guarantee of prevention in future of scandals such as payment protection insurance and of course Libor. It seems clear that a £300 million fine for a company generating several billion a year is no more than a slap on the wrist, especially when the concept of reputational damage does not really exist given how the man in the street already loathes the banking sector for a myriad of reasons.

Indeed, all that a fine tends to be is no more than a windfall tax which given the way that such business models work, will be paid by the retail customer above anyone else. But of course the retail customer was the main victim of Libor in the first place. But over and above the not killing the goose that lays the golden egg fine issue, there is another possible explanation apart from the regulator fining in order to fund its future/justify its existence. It is the way that given the nature of many complex financial instruments and practices, it would be almost impossible to get a jury to convict a Libor offender (apart from saying that they are greedy/horrible people), just as it would be next to impossible to get a jury to convict a fraudulent short seller who manipulates share price movements with malicious rumours regarding a company in order to drive it to financial destruction.

The fact that hardly anyone outside the professional arena and seasoned traders understands the concept of short selling means that those who profit from malicious share price declines, are immune from the legal process, in a way that insider traders on the long side can only dream of. (See also Lloyds Banking.)

2012 Price Action

The overall charting picture as far as Barclays for 2012 has been a 160p-260p range, a V shaped pattern centred around the Libor scandal bear trap dip, and the recovery for the shares from July via an inverted head and shoulders reversal. In fact, at the time when the stock was trading near the 160p zone the fear was that the Libor scandal would cause the bank "reputational" damage, something which of course we now know is ridiculous. It would be impossible for public/City opinion to sink any lower than it already had by that time regarding the sector – along the lines of Dracula being a failed blood donor I suspect. This meant that not wanting to buy into a toxic fundamental situation would probably have meant most traders ignored the 27 July double buy signal on the daily chart here. I say double signal on the basis that it was an end of day close back above the top of the 23 July gap down at 158p and the former initial July support at 158p. When you add in the bullish divergence support line in the RSI window backing up the technical buy argument, those who could ignore their fundamental fears had a humdinger of a buy combination signal.

But there was more. A new habit of mind in 2012 was to draw a support line from left to right across potential inverted head and shoulders reversals, as it solidifies the presence of the formation, and in turn builds confidence that a downtrend is coming to an end. Those who chickened out of going long of Barclays in the 160p's had a second bite of the cherry with the bounce off the right shoulder support line. Indeed, even waiting for an end of day close back above the 200 day moving average on the open of 9 September for a 206p would not have been a bad thing to do. This is because as the autumn progressed, and without even the need to test the blue 50 day moving average as support, Barclays was delivering an accelerating rally to the upside. This was forecast to hit the top of a rising trend channel from July as high as 300p by the start of 2013, all in all a remarkable recovery and something which underlines the Teflon nature of the stock and the sector as far as apparently negative influences.

Payoff

Although I have already hinted that Bob Diamond is perhaps not the type of person to be very high up on most Christmas card lists, this does not mean we should not look at the events of 2012 in a non-objective manner. Indeed, the way things panned out with the announcement of the Libor fixing fine, and the way that subsequently almost everyone seems to be involved in one way or the other, it can be said that actually Bob Diamond may not actually have had to resign. Ironically, we would look at the former CEO's cause rather more sympathetically given the way that he had the decency to resign. Oh yes, and he shouldn't have given up his bonus to the media/political lynch mob either. Indeed, the way we accelerated towards a witch hunt culture was one of the worst aspects of the past year – it is all about not just being guilty until proven innocent, but actually to prove the innocent guilty – as in the case of Lord McAlpine. By the time someone can defend themselves, the circus has already left town.

RBS: Direct Line To An IPO

The Set Up

In my opinion what is just as bad as living in a one party state/third world dictatorship, is living in a democracy that has delayed information on what is and what has been going on. While it can be argued that truth should be the first casualty of war, this concept is stretched on all the big issues – the fall of the Great British Banking sector in 2008 being one of them. I am afraid it is just useless to say as the Public Accounts Committee did in November 2012 that actually, by the way the £66bn spent on recapitalising Royal Bank of Scotland and Lloyds Banking Group is lost for good. It would have been better to say that in 2008 (as it was not too difficult to work out) . It could also be added that the UK banking sector lends too much in the boom times/doesn't lend when assets are cheap, doesn't pay much tax and we were better off with Building Societies. In addition, if the banks are/were allowed to go down then all the hot/shady money, laundered from gangsters, tax evaders and gun runners all over the world would not come to Britain to support the spiralling nation debt. It is not really too much to be ashamed of, just a cold, hard reality. Much in the way that the Association of British Insurers comments that High Street banks in the UK are becoming "uninvestable" due an interfering Government, obscure accounting practices and a snowstorm of regulatory reforms were no surprise. One presumes that the ABI were attempting a scare tactic, but with £1.5tln of financial firepower this is a bluff one hopes they will not be called on.

Moving onto RBS and as much as the selling coal to Newcastle float of Direct Line Insurance (DLG), the big highlight of 2012 had to be the emergence of the tax payer 82% owned group from the Asset Protection Scheme. This is the first big step on the road to normality from crisis mode, with the only things now left being the resumption of the dividend (not before 2015) and seeing how much Fred Goodwin's old group will have to pay as a slap on the wrist fine for its part in the Libor fixing scandal. But presumably after the £1.26bn statutory loss taken for the three months to September as reported in November, another few hundred million pounds for Libor should not create too much of a ripple.

2012 Price Action

The easiest thing to say about RBS during 2012 regarding its price action is that it was dominated by a trading range between 200p and 300p. While the sector being the teacher's pet in terms of government help and backing may have been one reason for the generally firm performance despite PPI and Libor, for RBS the run-up to the Direct Line Insurance float on 11 October marked a particularly sweet spot technically. This is said on the basis of the early September unfilled gap through the black 200 day moving average then around £2.33, the type of signal that one only sees in the strongest of charting situations. This was helped along at the beginning of October by a golden cross buy signal between the 50 and 200 day moving averages with the expectation-going into the start of 2013 being that at the very least the shares would end up no lower than £2.50 and as high as £3.20 plus. In fact, the longer the September gap remains unfilled, the greater the chance of 2012's range being the extended consolidation that leads to the share price rising significantly, 50% or more over the following year to 18 months.

Payoff

It is perhaps tempting to suggest that 2012 was the year when RBS shares climbed a wall of worry in the classic sense. However, it was actually year whereby despite issues such as PPI and Libor, the stock and the company were treated to rather good news-especially with regard to the exit from APS, and managing to get a decent IPO out of Direct Line Insurance. On this basis the relatively healthy performance of the shares over the past 12 months was very much more understandable, and once the Libor fines are out of the way it could be said that most of the negatives on the fundamental side will have been absorbed or essentially factored in.

Standard Chartered: From Here To Tehran

The Set Up

Those who love controversy were delighted in early August 2012 by the emergence of the Standard Chartered/Iranian money-laundering scandal – something to enliven the dull trading days of summer. While we live in an era of gaffes and scandals, the allegation that one of the UK's most haloed financial institutions was being dragged through the mud by an upstart New York lawyer attempting to achieve a career-making scalp in accusing the bank of a $250 billion deception was certainly something out of the ordinary. Even worse, until the dust settled this FTSE 100 company was as tarnished, in the same way in terms of being described as a rogue institution, as any Third World BCCI type company. Nevertheless, I presume that Benjamin Lawsky now operates from rather a larger office at the end of 2012 than he needed at the beginning. At least to date he has proved himself to be no Eliot Spitzer.

2012 Price Action

As can be seen on the daily chart of Standard Chartered before the upheaval in July, this is not normally a stock which causes any great stress to traders in terms of any white knuckle ride of volatility. Indeed, it can be seen that soon after the sell-off of 6-7 August, the shares recovered relatively quickly. But focusing in on the near-term chart of May to September, it is interesting from a charting perspective how many different formations and trading triggers that there actually are. For instance, one can see the key reversal to the downside of 6 August, the end of day close on 8 August at £13.15, just above the initial bear trap low of 1 June at £12.87, and finally the way that 7-14 August served up an island bottom reversal – effectively flagging the floor for the year in the stock. Perhaps the nastiest price action of the lot came with the combined gap fill days of 15 August and 21 August, effectively designed to ensure that whether long or short, almost any stop loss you can think of would have been hit. While there is no cure for such price action at the time, once you have realised that it has occurred, which would be within only a couple of sessions, you can then trade off these spikes knowing that you have gained knowledge of where the market is going by the financial sacrifice of others.

Payoff

In some ways the Standard Chartered debacle was Barclays Lite in the sense that as we already had the example of its fellow sector member coming on down, getting fined, and going on as normal, you did not have to be a Mensa member or perhaps more accurately a Chief Market Strategist to work out there would be a relatively happy slap on the wrist ending for Standard Chartered. Indeed, given the way that at the time of the nine-month update from the end of October, Standard suggested that profit growth had been cut to mid-single digits from a double digit range, it can be concluded that the $340 million fine may not have been exactly a price worth paying, but it clearly was not the end of the world. As was implied in the example of Barclays above, the way that the illegal transactions/market manipulation/mis-selling can be entirely cut out is if those involved lose the licence to operate, and perhaps just as importantly if those who regulate them also receive appropriate punishment. Clearly, if the FSA could be sued by RBS shareholders over the ABN Amro debacle, or those who nodded through the deal could face fines or jail terms, they would think rather more carefully before they decided to wave on or block such activities.

But in fact, all this really reminds us is over a quarter of a century after the City of London revolution known as Big Bang the only thing worse than self-regulation is having a regulator do it for you. Why the warning of caveat emptor and the civil courts cannot be used for those who have complained against a financial company instead of the millions wasted on regulatory red tape, remains an on-going mystery.

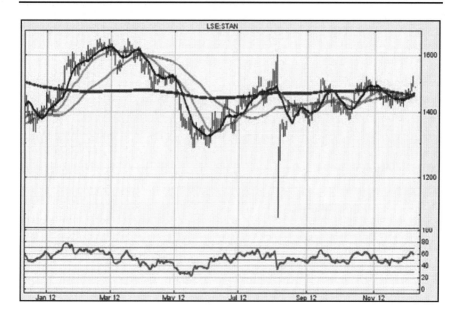

HSBC (HSBA): A Little Local Difficulty

The Set Up

I think it can be said quite fairly that the only thing worse than being taught the French language for ten years and not being able to speak even a sentence, is to be schooled in the dead language of Latin for 10 years and not being able to speak a word. There are of course some arguments for suggesting that French in the longer term – the next hundred years – might be in terminal decline in the manner of Latin. Of course, French is the language of the restaurant, and hence while we are talking a largely decorative purpose, it might just about survive!

However, it still seems important to exercise my French language muscle, such as when flying into Biarritz airport, which at least until very recently was emblazoned with advertisements for HSBC. If I remember rightly and have correctly translated, the world's local bank reminds us there that Turkey actually produces more wine than South Africa. But how cruel was fate to this bank in the choice of its advertising campaign in the sense that there can be nothing that underlines how clueless you are in a certain market to allow yourself to accept money laundered funds. I'm reminded of the way that just before its fall from grace to the discount/no-frills airlines such as Ryanair and easyJet, British Airways proclaimed itself to be the world's favourite airline. Ryanair now claims a similar world beating slogan for the web, after which you can bet your bottom dollar that the only way from there will be down.

But getting back to HSBC, and its 2012 scandal completed the full house as far as the UK banking sector is concerned and provided us, we the people, with the question we still need to answer: what in particular is it about banks which is so special, they are not allowed to fail? My view is that they are so entangled with the legal and political systems that if they were about to fall flat on their faces somehow the authority of government would be lost. But as I am only one of the apathetic millions I will leave it to the blogosphere/Twitterati to sort this out for me. In the meantime it may be worth remembering that the estimate of the amount of a charge HSBC would have to put aside for money-laundering was as much as $2 billion.

2012 Price Action

It strikes me that in general the term "elephants don't gallop" could have been made for HSBC in terms of the way that the price action of its share price tends to be very sluggish indeed. However, the year that the company was set to dive into its biggest scandal ever was one where the stock actually gapped to the upside in January, and reminded us of the January effect. It would appear that even when faced with a fundamental googly as HSBC did during the autumn of 2012, the share price action behaves as a law unto itself. That said, there were some key moments in the sense that the start of February saw a recovery of the black 200 day moving average then around the £5.55 level, with the following few weeks seeing repeated successful test for support by the stock at its falling 20 day moving average – usually such tests are a bullish sign. This led to a final end of June bear trap, with a significant low put in at 501p. But actually this was not the starting gun on the great rally in the stock. This came on 30 July with an end of day close back above the former 23 July gap down through the 200 day moving average. In this end of day close above the gap top was essentially the big signal near term, there was nothing else to know in terms of HSBC from that moment until towards the end of the year. Indeed the late 2012 price action is contained within a rising trend channel from July. What guided the stock north over H2 2012 was this channel and the way that all the near-term moving averages were rising higher in parallel, especially the blue 50 and the black 200 day lines. The fact that this channel was well above the 200 day line even on dips for the shares did emphasise the way that while the fundamental newsflow may have been rather dodgy at times, technical traders in the market were happy to scoop up HSBC stock.

Payoff

In the wake of the HSBC scandal which broke big-time in November, we were reminded that in the financial world through the course of the credit crunch, we have not so much had to choose between the good banks and the bad banks, good companies or the bad ones, but essentially involved in the battle to determine who was simply the least bad. At least in this respect one might have to say that HSBC is still a winner. We can also walk away with the reminder that since moral hazard and all its cousins, such as liberal guilt, were burned away rather early in the credit crunch crisis, these days it would appear that we are in a world where, as in no other time in history, anything goes. As a finale in terms of HSBC, it should also be noted that if such a big scandal is not enough to get the share price of a stock to wilt any more than the floor of its recent trading range levels, it is really rather difficult to think of a scenario where the worst could actually happen and a bank is destroyed in the manner of BCCI. Indeed, BBC/Jimmy Savile seems to be pushing the boundaries in terms of sin and taboo out to the limits in terms of any institution, financial or otherwise that can shake off any sin.

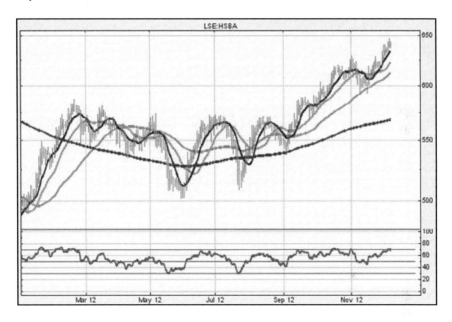

Lloyds: Culture Of Optimism

The Set Up

I have to admit that on a fundamental front Lloyds Banking did not exactly fire my imagination in 2012. Of course, there was the total (deliberate) PPI rip off cost set to hit £8bn, the Libor inquiries both in the UK and the US, and a £439m H1 loss, but nothing out of the ordinary for a part nationalised bank in the early 21st century. Nothing other than in November when it was revealed by HBOS's former head of risk in 2007-2008 Peter Hickman that short sellers "nearly" brought down the bank. Well, pal, they did enough to ensure that Lloyds Banking entered into a shotgun wedding with HBOS just months after the successful sabotage occurred in March 2008. Of course, no high profile prosecution for the bears, just a money wasting, too little, too late inquiry four years on. That said, the head of HBOS's corporate banking division Peter Cummings was banned for life and fined £500,000 by the FSA. Interestingly, our dear regulator pointed to a "culture of optimism" which led to the downfall of the bank. It does not get much more heinous than looking on the bright side in banking, does it?

2012 Price Action

I have to say that I did not really want to go back further than the start of 2012 for the chart snapshot of Lloyds Banking, but as can be seen by the trend lines drawn, not to do so would rather have spoilt the charting party. This is said on the basis that there has been a rising trend channel on the daily chart from approximately the start of September 2011, with the clear implication that the line resistance drawn from that point through the autumn 2011 highs is heading for a 50p target for early 2013. What can also be seen is that in October 2012 we were treated to a brief test of support through 37p – an area that had marked resistance for the shares for over a year. If anybody was in need of any confirmation that we are looking at a bullish situation here, the early October test for support was the technical backing they were looking for.

Payoff

What we learned about Lloyds Banking in 2012 was that we were being treated to not just an intermediate period of strength for the shares, but extended reversal most likely to lead to a major turnaround in share price. Somehow, quite magically the price action managed to laugh off any issues regarding Libor (everybody was involved in the scandal, and therefore it will be almost impossible and unfair to single any bank out), mis-selling of PPI, and of course the small matter of the 2011 annual loss of 3.5 billion pounds. Presumably the forecast of £3 billion profits arriving for 2012 and 2013 are the reason that even though many brokers are suggesting that the stock appears toppy, it should go to 50p and beyond early in 2013 – scandals permitting.

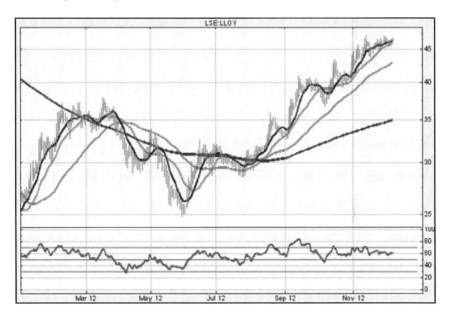

2012 Black Swans/White Swans: Key Stories

Bumi (BUMI): 100% Wrong

The Set Up

Bad name, bad result, and I am sure that whatever eventually happens Nat Rothschild's experience with Bumi will come a poor third to that of Jimi Hendrix and even Dame Edna Everage. Indeed, he was described as 100% wrong after resigning from the board of the Indonesian mining group on 15 October by the Deputy Chairman Sir Julian Horn-Smith in the wake of a proposed Bakrie family exit from Bumi. But at least on 5 November Rothschild produced some corporate fireworks of his own in delivering a counter offer to the Bakrie family. Perhaps the safest thing to say as this rather nasty corporate squabble continues is, watch this space. That said, it is not difficult to back Rothschild as the eventual winner, if there can be one after all the spitting of blood and share price wobbles we have seen in 2012.

2012 Price Action

As far as the stock market goes, the trend may be your friend, but sometimes you really can get too much of a good thing. This concept is underlined quite well on the daily chart of Bumi in the sense that we have a runaway move to the downside almost from the start of 2012. Indeed, it is punctuated by the odd temporary break above the 20/50 day moving averages. The general rule here would be to go short after any brief spike above the 50 day line, with the examples of the end of February, August and even October fitting the bill in this respect. From the chart there is also another signal, which is a general one of being short when parallel falling 50 day and 200 day moving averages are present. We can see this from the beginning of February and again towards the end of September. From a technical point of view it may be that the highlight of the year was one day in particular, 10 October, where the shares gapped up through £1.88 creating an island bottom reversal formation following the September exhaustion gap through 180p. Such a piece of price action should have delivered an almighty spike for the stock, and even though they managed to rise over 30% within two sessions it could be argued that given what a fantastic setup this was the shares should have gone a little higher than 300p. In fact the August-October snapshot also highlights another aspect of trading technically, this time with what is regarded as one of the better leading indicators, if not one of the few genuine examples of the genre. It can be seen in the oscillator window at the end of September there was a break below a RSI support line around the neutral 50 level which led the stock down from £3 to £1.50 and then at the beginning of October there was a break and RSI trendline leading the stock from around £1.60 to £3. I think these two signals are very important indeed in the sense that whenever you discuss technical analysis or charting with a traditional investor and they pick holes in this form of analysis, it is very unlikely that they will be familiar with this form of getting in ahead of time in a stock or market. I would say in the most genuine terms possible that correctly employed, and even with the odd cock up included, only trading on this basis, with the RSI oscillator, or others in the same series family such as the MACD or stochastic indicators, is really likely to give you an edge in the markets.

Payoff

For some reason there are few areas of conflict known to mankind that provide greater bad blood than a boardroom feud. We have seen this in the case of Mitchells and Butlers (MAB) and easyJet (EZJ) in the recent past, with the result being that public/shareholder opinion is polarised and it is very difficult not take sides. Given that in the case of Bumi we have a Rothschild involved, for many it may not be difficult to work out which side they wish to back. But either way, the best thing for this company in 2013 is for a return to normality. This is even if it means there is not quite some at excitement/volatility in terms of the share price.

Burberry (BRBY): China Proxy

The Set Up

From a trading perspective the attractions of Burberry, over and above any modelling Emma Watson may being doing for the luxury goods group, is that it is not difficult to regard the shares as being a China hard landing proxy. In fact, while I am a fan of the company on a fundamental basis as a long term growth story, it remains vulnerable to any hiccups in the Far East, and having wobbled already on the profits warning front you cannot help but think there is at least another one on the way, particularly if the Fiscal Cliff situation and/or China stimulus measures cannot keep GDP growth at 7% plus per annum.

2012 Price Action

Taking the first half of 2012 in the first snapshot of Burberry, it can be seen how the shares were flying almost from the start of January seeing support first coming in at the blue 50 day moving average and then above the 200 day moving average, a sign that this was a stock in prime bull mode. Indeed, from March there was a gap through initial February resistance at £14.64, another show of strength. What was interesting in terms of the full March/April pattern on the daily chart here is the way that there was essentially an island top within an island top. The particular stand out was the final three-day island top from the 12th to the 16th of the month, the signal that was also a narrow bull trap above the former March £15.86 intraday high. Adding to this combination of sell signals was the final one in May. Here the stock failed to deliver an end of day close back above the April island top gap at £15.61 peaking out at £15.48. From then on you might have expected it to be curtains for the stock, and this is more or less what we saw. However, it was a rather rocky ride, with £14 coming in as support in April, and £13 appearing to mark the bottom in May. But there was even more to come after the exhaustion gap to the downside in July was filled above £12.59 on 19 July. Following this the story here was that an August/early September island top above the blue 50 day moving average then standing just above £13 came into play. The gap down through the 50 day line on 10 September should have taken the shares on down for a fresh decline every bit as painful as that scene between April and July. But the longs were let off the hook by a very unusual cup and handle formation set against a vast gap to the downside which had its floor at £11.30. This became the base in terms of a hopeful salvation from Burberry shares – their equivalent of what the soft landing would be for the Chinese economy. At least from that moment on in late October the bulls knew that they had to fill the September gap through £13, which remains unfilled as of the end of November.

Payoff

Even going into 2012 it was the case that Burberry was the leading blue-chip proxy for the Chinese economy. This may be unfair given the geographical distribution of the business, but as even I was happy to make the link between China soft landing/hard landing and the luxury goods group, this link is one that will last quite some time. This is particularly the case given that I do not believe that China will be able to avoid its GDP growth heading below 5% over the next couple of years, even if the great miracle in its economy revives after that. As for Burberry, it is a long-term growth story, but the China wobble factor needs a little more time to play out, perhaps even longer than the next year.

Mulberry (MUL): Poor Man's Burberry

The Set Up

As far as shares in Mulberry are concerned it could be argued that 2012 really started in December last year, indeed on 21 December when Panmure Gordon delivered some pre-Christmas cheer regarding the luxury fashion brand. It reiterated its buy recommendation on the occasion of a new Chief Executive being appointed, on the basis that this would gear that group up for global growth. To be fair, this enthusiasm was actually born out towards the end of January this year when Mulberry raised its full-year forecasts on profits having achieved a solid Christmas performance. Unfortunately, after this point I can deliver very little more on the fundamental front, given that my knowledge of the subject begins and ends with an irrational hatred of the manbag.

2012 Price Action

One of the points that seem difficult for me to resist in the two years since I wrote *101 Charts* is that the exercise has really accelerated and solidified the way I use charting techniques, and what I use. Mulberry provides a good example of this in the sense that we have a couple of the most high-profile and favourite charting events evident here. The first is the unfilled gap just above the black 200 day moving average at the end of January, something which in my post-*101 Charts* period has become one of the most favoured and most reliable signs that a stock or market is set for a massive move to the upside. But perhaps the biggest point to note here is actually that while bull runs start in this fashion, big selloffs do not have the inverse version of this – something which is clearly one of life's great mysteries. As far as the price action aspect of Mulberry is concerned I would prefer to say that from January to June, and up to the day of the June gap to the downside there was very little reason for bulls of the stock to consider taking profits. While it has to be admitted that there was clear bearish divergence between the April and May price highs in the RSI window, a double bear trap prior to the gap down in the middle of June meant that it was not a done deal that one should exit on the long side of Mulberry shares. This is even though in the three sessions prior to the 14 June gap down we had a triple failure below the blue 50 day moving average. Essentially, what I am trying to say is that while the mid-June gap to the downside was a massive sell signal, it is not difficult to imagine that there were many longs caught out by the move. Indeed, the evidence that people had been caught long of Mulberry is the very size of the gap down, and the way that it was a gap down through the 200 day moving average, now established as a very strong sell signal/trend changing event. As far as what happened for the rest of the year the points to note here were the way that the price action was so massively below the 200 day moving average, as well as the way that from the autumn onwards even the 50 day moving average all but caps the price action. The main issue going into the end of the year was essentially whether the former September intraday support at £11 would remain as the resistance cap on the stock? Going into November the only real plus point here was the way that bullish divergence appeared to be developing in the RSI window, although even in the wake of this one would regard only an end of day close back above £11 as the minimum initial buy signal. By 26 November the best Mulberry had achieved was a November intraday high of £10.99.

Payoff

Although it feels somewhat trite to suggest that Mulberry is a poor man's Burberry, the profits warnings and share price plunges of June and October rather suggest that unless the stock can dig itself out of its current fundamental and technical hole it may be a while before we see it entering the FTSE 100 club. This is especially the case if you believe the old stock market adage that the profits warnings come in threes, with two down, and one apparently still to go.

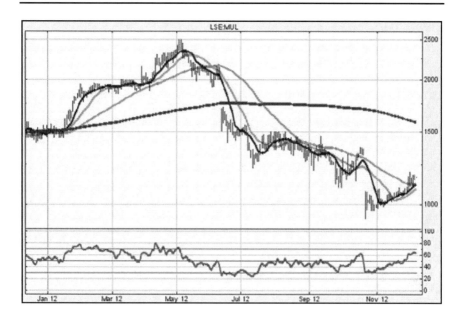

G4S (GFS): Don't Mention The Olympics

The Set Up

I presume that I am not the only one who when someone mentions an armed robbery will immediately think of a Securicor van, or when prisoners escape while in transit, Group 4. Luckily, the merger of Group 4 with Securicor to create G4S in 2004 erased such issues, until now. Henceforth G4S will always be tainted with the London 2012 Olympics security fiasco. That said the failed ISS deal the year before and associated costs did effectively flag this company as somewhat wobbly on the fundamental front, as did reported periodic mishaps with G4S security in recent years. A fresh name change seems overdue: I am putting forward S4Security . . .

2012 Price Action

One can assume that no one knew that there was going to be a fiasco regarding the Olympics, or indeed could have known. But looking at the chart of G4S leading into July, it can be said that the price action is jittery to say the least. While at least nominally there may be a £2.70-£2.90 range, the turning points are bull and bear traps, and are almost always vertical. Perhaps the highlight before July is the May island bottom bear trap below the black 200 day moving average below £2.65. This gave us a very encouraging buy signal going into the summer debacle, one which could have easily led to a break to the upside and 300p plus had fate not intervened. Instead, we had a very catchable decline. This is said on the basis of the early July narrow bull trap just above the former April £2.89 peak. Indeed, one could have gone short on the first end of day close back below £2.89 which was on 12 July at £2.83. The stop loss then would have been an end of day close back above the gap to the downside at £2.87 on 11 July. So in this instance one would have been perfectly in position ahead of a gap through the 200 day moving average on 16 July. In fact, the only problem with G4S in relation to the big gap down sell signal through the 200 day line is the way that rather than marking the start of a major move to the downside, even going into the autumn the shares merely formed new resistance from old support around the £2.70 level but never broke down fully.

Payoff

The G4S saga may have been a bolt from the blue if you were Nick
Buckles, but at least it can be said on a technical basis that this was a
situation to be profited from using technical analysis techniques. Perhaps
the real message is that while the G4S management may have goofed, the
Olympics did not suffer due to the replacement of non-English-speaking
security staff, and the estimated £50 million loss while significant was far
from being a mortal blow to a company the size of G4S. Perhaps this is
why the CEO, Nick Buckles, a man with arguably the best hair in the FTSE
100, still remains at the helm.

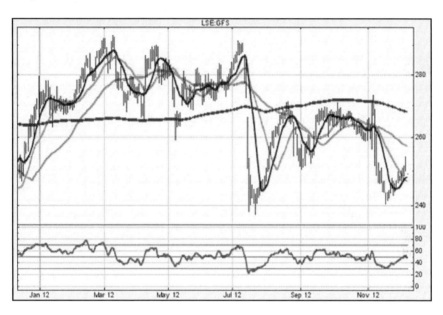

Lonmin (LMI): South African Woes

The Set Up

The usual tone of what I write has a cynical, perhaps even blasé tone even without any effort at all. In the case of events at South Africa focused miner Lonmin in the second half of 2012 the description of a nightmare scenario unfolding is really the only perspective to take. The mixture of business and politics in South Africa appear to have become a fatal one, with no likely end in sight as miners have apparently become the pawns in this situation. 34 were killed in August by South African police, causing international outcry and bringing Lonmin to its knees financially. Unfortunately, the end of October rights issue might be a temporary sticking plaster, unless there is a fundamental change in South Africa's mining sector and/or its politics. The revelation that Lonmin rejected a bid from Xstrata (XTA) in September could be taken as a move that effectively gave the thumbs down to an orderly reversal of the ongoing meltdown in the group's prospects.

2012 Price Action

Although the way that shares of Lonmin almost exactly halved peak to trough in 2011 from £10 to £5 might have made some in the market think that all and any bad news had been factored into the price, events at Marikana ensured that this could not possibly be the case. The big giveaway on the negative side early in 2012 was the triple failure for the share price at and just below the falling 200 day moving average then above £5.50. This really was an extended sell signal, with the unfilled gap down of 14 May underlining the negative momentum building up. But perhaps what is more intriguing on this chart is if we forward through to the autumn where despite positive RSI divergence the stock made a new low for the year under £2.50. The message after this is that if a stock/market cannot rebound with such a strong back up, the technical outlook really is for a tailspin to follow imminently unless something very special happens technically.

Payoff

Perhaps the main issue with Lonmin in recent months has been the temptation to think of the stock as a possible bottom fishing opportunity just because it has fallen so far. As things stand this does not appear to be the case, especially while we see no sustained price action back above the old September floor at £2.79. We are just getting this at the end of November 2012, but without the prospect of any real fundamental positives likely to emanate from South Africa over the first part of 2013, it is difficult to see how a rally can be sustained much beyond September's 380p peak.

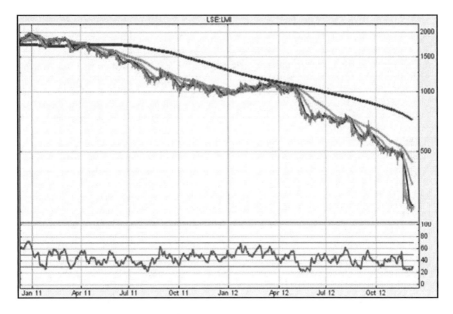

Ocado (OCDO): Still Off Its Trolley

The Set Up

I have to admit that on a fundamental basis at least I have spent much of 2012 not being particularly kind to the apparently and inadvertently profits adverse business model of Ocado. This follows on from the mauling the group received in *101 Charts* from 2010. The latest newsflow as of late November 2012 was that while Ocado is heading for a banking covenants breach, its creditors very kindly offered it a Greece-style debt payment extension. Delaying the inevitable perhaps, especially after a £35.8m cash raising event, but give a rival real world grocer the chance to buy Ocado and put it out of its and my own misery.

That said, if by some magic spell I was made CEO of the online grocer, there is little doubt that I would be singing its praises as a revolutionary concept, as revolutionary as the introduction of supermarkets to the United Kingdom 50 years ago. Nevertheless, it would appear that whatever the merits of the group are, it will always be up against it in terms of the stranglehold existing players have in its sector, the economies of scale advantages that they have, and the way that essentially they could simply turn up the heat to price Ocado out of business. What will be interesting to 2013 is whether the dreaded C word, (banking) covenant, comes into play as it did on at least one occasion this year. To my mind it would appear that the best scenario here is if one of the existing trolley-pushing sector members merges with Ocado, or trying to be extremely creative there is a takeover by the likes of Amazon (AMZN). Come to think of it, why doesn't Ocado go for non-food items delivery as well and try and beat Amazon at its own game?

2012 Price Action

While some might be wondering how a relatively small company, with relatively run-of-the-mill newsflow attracts so much attention, I suppose the answer comes from the prospect of it breaking its banking covenant and because the stockmarket is supermarkets obsessed. But at least we saw the share price of Ocado get off to a flyer at the start of 2012 – presumably in hope that the worst days for the group were finally behind it in terms of sales/demand. Of course, all the year-end tipsters missed out on suggesting that Ocado would be one of the most promising plays for 2012 , at least initially. The technical trigger was a bear trap low on 11 January combined with bullish divergence in the RSI window. This led to a very impulsive looking move to the upside consisting of no less than four stages in which the share price more than doubled over a period of not much more than eight weeks. In fact, there was actually more to come in the form of a double-headed head and shoulders between February and June, with the end of the line for the bulls 2012 essentially coming with a 26 June gap to the downside that melted the 200 day moving average then already falling below 100p. The problem is that from that point onwards, especially in the wake of the July dead cross between the 50 and 200 day moving averages, the prospects for the longs started to look increasingly grim. Indeed, it would be easy to say that while there is no weekly close back above post-July 80p resistance, bears of Ocado have every reason to be licking their lips, even after the November debt deal. The chief reason is the way that pre-July support was at 90p, a full 10p above the highs that have followed. This support-resistance difference or gap, is any seen in the most bearish of situations, given the way that the shares have had months to close it and have not been able to do so a sub-50p target and possibly much worse seem to be on the cards for 2013.

Payoff

Clearly one of the remits of *Lessons* is to focus on what happened between 1 January and 31 December 2012, and in the case of Ocado it seems particularly apt to use this and go for making a call on the prospects for 2013. Clearly, such a sticking out of the neck would only be done for a compelling situation, and in the case of Ocado the bears have worries over cash burn as well as a support resistance gap on their side. Indeed, at this stage the only way that a negative call on the shares could come undone would be if the group has a fantastic Christmas 2012 and/or is taken over.

Supergroup (SGP): New Challenges

The Set Up

One of the more bizarre pieces of newsflow of the year was the announcement by Supergroup co-founder Theo Karpathios of his resignation in August to "take on new challenges". This was quite a bolt from the blue, and not only on the basis that even being the first man to walk on Mars would be less of a challenge than getting the share price of the "Superdry" brand owner back to the glory days of 1,800p plus at the start of 2011. In other words, something did not quite gel. This is especially so given the way that only weeks beforehand the group had announced a 15% profits decline.

2012 Price Action

While it might sound ridiculous to suggest that for Supergroup in 2012 we saw one of the most remarkable charting journeys that one could wish to see, such a statement may at least convey the amount of action crammed into a relatively short space of time. The kick-off with the special price action at the start of February, both in the form of bearish divergence in the RSI window between the January and February price highs, followed by a mini island top reversal one that flags a move down towards the 500p zone. But it was perhaps the £5.69 low in April under the initial £5.72 support that led to one of the more spectacular breakdowns of the year. In fact, truth be told it also led to a rare failure of a bullish divergence buy signal at the start of May as indicated by the red line in the RSI window. By failure what is meant is that there was not a clear push to the upside. Instead there was a mild recovery, followed by a gradual keeling over into a bear trap as low as £2.65, something which proved to be the low zone of the year. Happily this was flagged by bullish divergence in the RSI window between April and June support, and Supergroup was off to the races in a way that we have not seen for a couple of years.

I think it is fair to call this it a cup and handle formation, even though for all practical intents and purposes we were dealing with a break of the middle of a lopsided W-shaped reversal. An end of day close back above the July 498p intraday peak was a mighty buy signal, and Supergroup did not let the buyers down. Indeed just in case anyone was a digitally regarding the prospects for the share price over the autumn, this was reiterated by a golden cross between the blue 50 and black 200 day moving averages and missed September, as well as the on-going support at a RSI uptrend line in place from the middle of June. I would then suggest that actually this RSI window feature with the multi-tested rising trendline reflected how strong the recovery for the trendy company's shares really was.

Payoff

If nothing else, ever since it came to market one can say that Supergroup has provided technical and indeed, fundamental traders with almost every form of entertainment you could wish for, apart from say, a boardroom feud. With the shares topping out near 700p once again towards the end of 2012 it remains to be seen whether for the near term the best of the recovery that 2012 brought is over. The problem is that sub 700p still leaves the door open for more whiplash inducing price action with a 300p-700p range that dominated 2012, due for 2013.

Tesco (TSCO): Averaging Down

The Set Up

Given the way that shares of Tesco are normally such a quiet market, you really have to be on your toes to start 2012 in terms of being prepared for the seismic activity in the price action. What is clear in the wake of the generally the twelfth warning from the group is that we were looking at a major shift on the fundamental front, confirmed in terms of deception. This meant that for many the UK's number one supermarket was no longer the golden fleece but instead was a shining example of the emperor's new clothes. Even though the world's greatest investor Warren Buffett is involved in the stock and indeed bought more in the wake of the profits warning in January, even he had to average down, it may be that unless the group can pull something quite magical out of the hat, he may have to average down again. This would be the case especially if the supermarket sector in the UK in the next decade starts to resemble the UK political scene in that there is increasingly less difference between the major players. It may also be the case that even if one of the leading supermarket groups adopts a strategy which gives it an edge over its peers, this is whittled away so quickly in the current environment that the kind of lead Tesco enjoyed during the 1990s and 2000s is unlikely to be seen again. This would clearly be bad news in terms of profits and share price/rating of the company.

2012 Price Action

Perhaps the most important interest in terms of the January Gap Down from the daily chart of Tesco is the way that such a signals normally conspire to ensure that a stock or market that suffers it will be in bear mode for typically six months to a year. What this means is that the top of the gap, in this case at £3.83, will be in place as lasting resistance for the shares. Indeed, it is the case normally that the only way of reversing such a chronic bearish signal is a gap back up through the 200 day line. As far as what happened in 2012 after Tesco's charting shock, it can be said that in terms of the bearishness we are looking at an 8/10 on the doomed scale. This is said on the basis that any rebound for the stock peaked well below the bottom of the gap at £3.63. There was also a September bull trap through the March £3.41 resistance, as well as an August to October bull trap through the falling 200 day moving average itself. This litany of misery actually suggests that there will be a new gap down towards the end of 2012 or even let us say in January again to mark the anniversary of the first sell-off. While in theory weekly close back above the 200 and moving average might be an excuse to start bottom fishing, on this occasion it may be wise to simply err on the side of missing a potential recovery rather than joining the herd which has already been attempting to find a floor in a value stock, but instead has so far become mired in the price action equivalent of quicksand.

Payoff

The intuitive thing to do here at Tesco as far as most traders were concerned, was and is, to be in bottom fishing mode. However, the gap down below the 200 day moving average is an unequivocal signal not to do so, even if there may be near-term dead cat bounces in the stock prices. Given the ongoing failure to close the 2012 gap, and the fresh failure back below the 200 day moving average, selling into strength rather than weakness remains the mantra unless we are treated to a clear higher low back above the 200 day line by the end of 2012.

Glencore (GLEN): GlenStrata Is Formed

The Set Up

Although there is perhaps not so much glory in insisting that you are one of the people who regard the Glencore IPO as a turkey right from the start, much in the way that the share price high for Facebook was on day one, at least this for the former was an idea I can claim. The call was predominantly on the basis of it being clear to me that by the time the mining giant came to the market in May 2011, we were already just coming off the top of a particularly strong phase for mining stocks/precious metals. Indeed as things stand, we will probably require gold to not only take out its 2012 resistance above $1900, but also by some distance in order to get the same kind of fever/mania year for mining shares that we had last year.

As far as the story of Glencore during 2012 was concerned, we had a well flagged merger on the cards with Xstrata (XTA), with the feeling being that this was something of a forced marriage, rather than one where there were compelling reasons to get together apart from the obvious synergies.

2012 Price Action

If nothing else the price action progression for Glencore over 2012 illustrates why the powers that be at the mining group might have wished to get together with Xstrata. In fact despite the January-February and then July-August rallies for the share price the falling 200 day moving average ensured that even the most ardent fan of the company itself and of the Glenstrata idea, would not have been happy. Also not helping anyone remain in good cheer were two failed breakouts through the 200 day moving average, one at the end of April, the other at the beginning of September. But it can often be said in the wake of such brief traps that depending on how far the price action can penetrate the 200 day line we are looking at either the start of a recovery or the continuation of an extended chronic group to the downside. As always you have to check for additional technical backing. Perhaps the only real glimmer in terms of the early autumn daily chart of Glencore was the way that a trendline trap can be drawn through from May support at £3.30. On the basis of this snapshot it would be surprising if the stock could not manage to retest the former 400p September intraday high zone well before the end of 2012. But it has to be acknowledged that the head and shoulders reversal failure at the 200 day moving average is not an event that can be shaken off easily, and therefore it would be perfectly understandable if would be buyers here simply decided to stand back until there was sustained and extended price action back above the 200 day line.

Payoff

Given that this is the mining sector it may be appropriate to wheel out what is a rather appropriate phrase (verging on a pun), in suggesting that as far as the Glencore/Xstrata M&A story goes for 2012, all that glitters has certainly not been gold. We appear to be in a period where even the most obvious of deals are subject to so much regulatory, shareholder and general speculation and noise, that they drag on so long, meaning that whatever enthusiasm there was initially is long gone by the time the ink is dry on any deal.

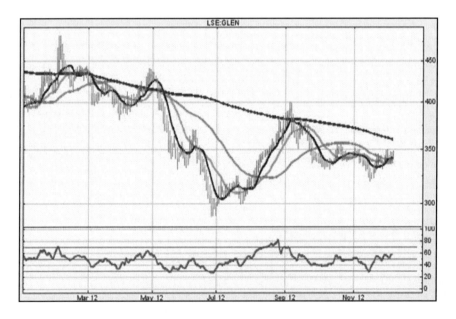

Xstrata (XTA): A Merger of Equals

The Set Up

Basically, there are two things that you know for certain when you hear that a "merger of equals" is being created, as was reported in February 2012. The first is that the two companies involved are certainly not equal, and the second is that the deal should probably not be happening at all. Being armed with such wisdom for the rest of the year was probably the way to go, especially given all the headwinds that the idea of Glenstrata was buffeted with. Ahead of the deal being finally "waved" through at the end of November it was a case of everyone who could grumble/block the deal, including even retail investors, was keen to do so. No wonder the amount of M&A these days has totally dried up.

2012 Price Action

It seems fair and logical to proceed on the assumption that the price action of Xstrata in recent months has been all too similar to that of Glencore. In fact it is easier to talk about the few differences between Xstrata and Glencore than the similarities. The main one is the way that at the start of February Xstrata shares jumped violently to the upside, with a gap down at the beginning of March delivering an island top reversal formation which correctly forecast the decline for much of the rest of the year. In fact, while the formation of the March island top delivered an initial £1.50 downside, enough to satisfy most traders, the best signal of the year was the way that at the end of April the top of the March £11.90 to gap was filled leading to a £3 decline to what turned out to be the lows of the year under £8. The worst aspect of 2012 price action arguably came during September when an inverted head and shoulders reversal in place on the daily chart from May through to the end of August ended up being eight bull traps through the 200 day moving average. What should have happened is that there was a retest of the late April resistance through £12, but the actual confirmation of the merger with Glencore apparently was enough to blow such a scenario out of the water.

Payoff

While there was clearly plenty of excitement surrounding the prospects of Glenstrata being formed in mid-2012, the shenanigans associated with the deal, as well as no doubt much behind-the-scenes activities, rather took the edge off the whole affair. In the case of Xstrata, as in the example of Glencore above, the immediate post-merger atmosphere is definitely biased to the bullish side, something which is rather surprisingly given the relative lack of enthusiasm we saw along the way during most of 2012 courtship for the two companies. If the deal proves to be a success, and the share price does not start to soar, it may actually be because this event has coincided with an upturn in the mining sector's rally within the market, and relief that China may not be imploding as badly as previously feared.

BAE Systems (BA.): In Need of EADS

The Set Up

After the failure of the BAE Systems/EADS deal in early October, it was the Financial Times that suggested in all its wisdom that BAE Systems is a sitting duck for a takeover. While this may be the case in theory, especially after the botched EADS, it could just as easily be argued that if BAE could not be soldered with EADS, the prospects of anyone else being willing to step forward in order to get an extended serious headache regarding regulatory, political and even logistical matters do not seem great.

That said, it cannot be denied that BAE Systems is in need of a shakeup and a fresh lease of life. Perhaps the Germans who have been blamed by the financial press for the failure of the deal (we can blame them for everything) can come up with a solution? They may need to come up with something in a timely manner, given the way that we are living in scandal hungry times, and we are once again overdue a gripe in the financial press regarding human rights abuses in the countries that BAE sells arms to, and of course there is the question of bribes. If I was in charge of communications at the defence contractor I would be happy to suggest that you cannot make an omelette without cracking an egg or two, so that it is just as well that I have not been headhunted in this respect as yet. I would maintain though, that if there is war and conflict and the need for countries to defend themselves, I would prefer it if British companies were engaging in what is an unavoidably dirty business, rather than anyone else. It would be wonderful if such services were not required, but we do not live in a fairy tale world, and adopting a naive stance doesn't help anyone either. Perhaps giving the United Nations some teeth would.

2012 Price Action

Those who are familiar with the price action/share price trading levels of BAE Systems over the years will be aware as I am that as a general rule anywhere below 300p for the stock is on the cheap side. Therefore the loss of this zone at the end of March did flag the possibility that something was going on, or could happen on a fundamental basis given the way that the shares will now in theory be in the bargain basement zone. As can be seen on the daily chart the question was the technical spectre of whether the stock would find support at the black 200 day moving average, then just under £2.90. In fact it did not, meaning we were confronted with the prospect of a possible extended decline, at least if you were working on the basis of just the events in the price window. What flagged a floor in the shares though, was extended bullish divergence in the RSI window between April support just below £2.90 and May support just below £2.70. Given the 20p difference to have a higher RSI support zone was actually quite remarkable. The final buy trigger as far as the price chart was concerned came in the form of a narrow bear trap low on 25 May, from which the grey 20 day moving average then essentially guided the stock higher over the coming months. Nevertheless, it is worth mentioning that there was an initial June bull trap through the 200 day moving average then at £2.89, meaning that those trading the stock probably had to enjoy being stopped out at least once before finally getting on an extended move. The starting gun for this was a 29 June gap through the blue 50 day moving average, a classic buy signal, with the point to be noted being the way that this gap down to £2.81 remains unfilled to this day. Just as important, in terms of what the longevity of the extended recovery could be/is both the multi-tested falling RSI support line from July, and the way that since the start of that month we have been treated to multiple support points well above the 200 day moving average. Of course, it helped build confidence that the early August golden cross buy signal between the 50 and 200 day moving averages did deliver the goods in terms of taking the stock from around the £3.15 mark to £3.60 in less than a month, and do so in an unusually nonvolatile fashion.

Payoff

While the lack of a merger in 2012, and no exit (merger) route, BAE Systems may have left many traders rather frustrated on a fundamental perspective, although from the technical angle things were rather more satisfactory. The dip below the 200 day moving average in May and then the gap through the 50 day moving average the following month, provided a reasonably straightforward pair of setups for a stock which is normally fiddly historically as the price action tends to be rather flat. The best scenario for the start of 2013 would be that the shares have already consolidated as an above the former February £3.34 resistance zone, so that a lasting break of resistance in the £3.60 zone can be achieved. The good news is that if we see a new instance of a monthly close back above 360p there is little in the way of charting furniture to be hit until 500p plus, last seen in 2008.

Britvic (BVIC): Going Soft

The Set Up

Soft (very sugary) drinks group Britvic may be most famous to us as the supplier of the orange that goes in a vodka and orange, but it could be said that as far as the stock market is concerned interest stems from the way that ever since the shares came to the stock market in their current form six years ago, the group appeared to be a slam dunk takeover target. It seemed quite obvious that the likes of Diageo, Coca-Cola, Pepsi, et al would have wanted swallow up Britvic for their respective portfolios. Instead, you would have had to wait for more than half a decade for Irn-Bru group AG Barr to step up to the plate. Of course, while I am delighted that a company from the (soon to be independent) country of my birth has decided to do the honours in the form of a merger, there is not quite the excitement in the deal that that there could have been. This may be said on the basis that the origins of the tie-up with AG Barr stemmed from the 11 July announcement of a recall of its Robinsons Fruit Shoot and Fruit Shoot Hydro drinks which was forecast to cost as much as 25m pounds. The associated profits warning on the forecast that full-year results would be at the bottom end of market expectations almost certainly meant that for the management of Britvic, seeking out a partner – or not saying no to any offers – appeared to be the best way forward.

2012 Price Action

Although I just wanted to focus on the 2012 price action here, there can be seen that there is a material reason for including snapshot wide enough to take in 2011 as well. This is said on the basis that the big buy signal here in 2012 came on the wall of an end of day close back above the August 2011 intraday low of £2.84. Indeed the buy signal in July was a reversal gap fill. This payroll of 19 July in the form of an end of day close at £2.95, after which it was effectively an easy ride for the stock for a spike in early September above £3.80. Indeed from that point on, one could use the 200 day moving average towards £3.50 as end of day close trailing stop loss.

Payoff

An interesting point to note there is the way that for much of the autumn the stock still struggled to get up to the 400p plus highs of early 2012, before the merger was announced. On this basis it could be argued that those in the know here were anticipating some kind of M&A activity well ahead of time. Admittedly, this could have been said regarding Britvic for several years now.

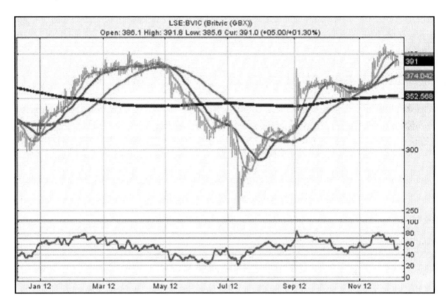

Heroes of the FTSE 100

ARM Holdings (ARM): Ever The Hero

The Set Up

To my mind there was really only one hero stock as far as the FTSE 100 that really fitted the bill in a relatively lacklustre year, and it was chip designer ARM Holdings. In fact I was quite gushing about the company a couple of years back in *101 Charts*, and given the way that the gadget/mobile/smartphone revolution has continued to balloon ever since, you can imagine that my enthusiasm remains. Indeed, this view remains stronger than ever even after the recent carnage as far as Apple shares are concerned, on the old adage that those who make the most out of a Gold Rush are not the miners, but those who make the shovels and pick axes. On this basis ARM's fundamental future appears to be very much a rosy one. The highlight of the year, the best day, came on 23 October with the announcement that third quarter profits more than doubled to £43m.

2012 Price Action

The gap higher for ARM shares in the wake of the Q3 update left a third unfilled gap on the daily chart since 15 October, and less than a month later there were four unfilled gaps. Given that two unfilled gaps in close proximity are usually only seen in the most bullish of situations, it is not surprising that at the time I described ARM as being the proud owner of the strongest blue chip chart of the year. What can be said going into the last month of 2012 is that even though ARM shares have come up a long way already, and appear overstretched as much on a fundamental financial ratios basis, as on the technicals, while above the floor of gap number three this autumn at 695p the upside here should be as great as the 750p level, equating to the top of a rising trend channel from July, by the end of January.

Payoff

Although there is a little ARM in almost every smartphone on the planet, it would not be wise to do an "Apple" and calculate that 2+2=5. Instead, we have a decent breakout for ARM shares, and while this should continue well into 2013, we should not assume that it will not be a rocky ride.

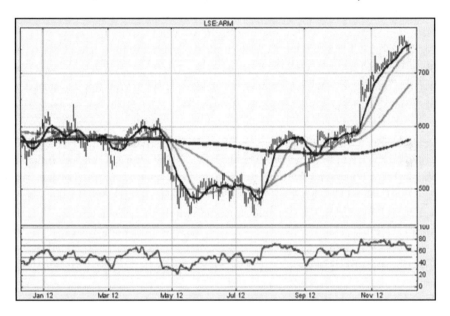

Imperial Tobacco (IMT): Fire Without Smoke

The Set Up

Being such a libertarian, and of course middle-aged enough not to be politically correct, I believe that people have a right to smoke anywhere. I also believe that there are worse crimes in the world than smoking a cigarette indoors in a public place, and that's my opinion whether I'm a smoker or not. For instance, how can you have a proper pub without a pall of smoke hanging over the bar? Unfortunately for companies like Imperial Tobacco the anti-right to choose/overregulation lobby, otherwise known as the killjoys with nothing meaningful to do in their life, regard smoking and its passive form as being a truly abhorrent activity. Ordinarily, I would agree with them, if only on the basis of cancer alone. However, we have lost so many rights and liberties over the past 30 years, and have Big Brother watching us almost everywhere, that although it may be foolishly masochistic to say so, cancer might be regarded as a price worth paying.

2012 Price Action

While it is the case that Imperial Tobacco has gone on and on as a potential takeover target, with the newsflow in 2012 reflecting the perennial nature of such speculation, it can be said that from a charting perspective the prospect of such a M&A scenario appeared rather less likely, if anything, than in recent years. This is said primarily on the basis of March-July delivering a quadruple failure at just above the £26 level. While one could not go on to rule out the break of such hefty resistance, it is hardly a surprise that for the second half of 2012 we saw shares of Imperial struggle to make headway. Indeed, 5 September witnessed a classic gap down below the 200 day moving average, something which implies that while there was no end of day close back above the gap top £24.37 one would be happy as a seller into strength. In fact, if you step back from the daily chart price pattern of the year for the shares you are confronted with a rounded top reversal. This not only rules out a takeover, it suggests an extended bear market for Imperial Tobacco. This would imply that only a takeover of the group, i.e. fundamental intervention, could cancel out what is a very bearish looking chart.

Payoff

Something which is a standard as far as the daily chart progression at Imperial Tobacco over the past year is the way that it would normally be the case that there is an element of doubt regarding the prospects for a takeover at a company on the basis of the price action/technical. In this situation we have a clear message from the chart that no bid is expected. While of course there is nothing to prevent a third party turning up with cash on the table to provide Imperial shareholders with a pleasant surprise, the way the stock has been traded implies that those in the know have actually been heading for the exit here, rather than trying to get on the bandwagon of any potential deal.

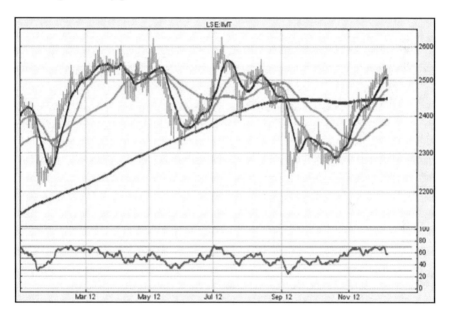

M&S (MKS): Bid Rumours Remain

The Set Up

Although M&S shares belong to a traditionally sedate sector, and potentially the most dramatic thing that could happen is that there is a run on ladies underwear, the price action here is deceptively noisy. While the average true range in the recent past has normally been less than 10p, it would appear from a visual inspection of whatever position is taken, whether it is long or short, you have to be prepared for a swing against you from the entry point of as much as 20p even if you are proven correct on the trade. Therefore, going long of the stock on reports in the financial media of a takeover can mean that the first thing you know after a couple of sessions is that a generous 20p or even 30p stop loss has been hit.

2012 Price Action

Let us say that for the bulk of 2012 M&S shares occupied a relatively wide range between 300p and 400p. In fact, the original impetus for the 2012 rally came from a November 2011 bear trap, with the single during 2012 coming in the form of a golden cross between the grey 20 and blue 50 day moving averages. It has to be admitted now that this was not exactly a compelling invitation to go long given the way that normally M&S shares do not pack much of a punch for any given signal even a decent one such as the 20/50 day golden combination. Indeed, it could be argued that the best technical signals here came a little later in the year. The first one was April's gap down through the blue 50 day moving average, where the 50 day line could have been used as the end of day close stop loss prior to the summer's at £3.20 lows. But it was the second one in the form of the July double bull trap below June £3.19 support that proved to be as good as double bear traps (or double bull traps) normally are. In fact if you look closely you can see how 27 July was a gap up day and great buy signal while there was no end of day close back below £3.25. For the rest of the year there was the support of an extended May RSI uptrend line, which was a multi-tested feature, a September golden cross buy signal between the blue 50 day and the black 200 day moving averages, as well as new support points well above the 200 day line from August onwards. Indeed on this basis one could say at least from a technical perspective that if nothing was going to happen on the takeover front, it was difficult to believe that this would be the case.

Payoff

M&S this year has been noteworthy at least a couple of ways. Firstly in the way that it reminds us of how even the most gentle of markets can provide quite evil near-term price action volatility, and second how you can use technical analysis and charting methods to determine whether, or even how likely it is that a major fundamental event such as a takeover bid could be forthcoming in the near-term.

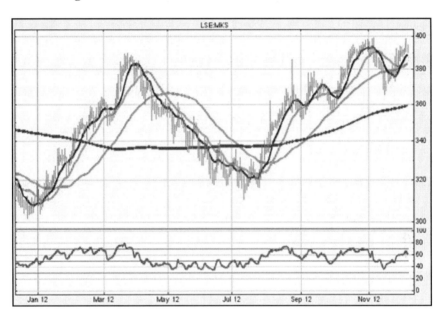

Sage (SGE): A Wise Tech Play

The Set Up

Perhaps one of the most striking differences that there remains between the US and UK stock markets is the relative lack of new economy plays on this side of the Atlantic. Indeed, after the takeover of Autonomy by Hewlett Packard (HPQ) in August 2011, really we are back to just having ARM Holdings (ARM) as our one truly exciting technology play. That said, Autonomy has become even more exciting after the takeover that it was beforehand. Of course, Sage is in the FTSE 100 and certainly not be sniffed at, but accountancy software does not quite grab the imagination in the way that Autonomy's knowledge management software did, or ARM's chip designing for the likes of Apple (AAPL) still do. Nevertheless, we live in hope, and in the meantime it would be pleasant to see a takeover finally materialise to light up the price action packed Sage. For 2012 the main candidate in this respect was Germany's software giant SAP.

2012 Price Action

We have been treated to a rather intriguing charting year as far as Sage shares are concerned, something which is said on the basis of the way that this market managed to float above both its 50 day and 200 day moving averages for the first couple of months of 2012. But the real plus points here were charting signals in the form of the May gap down just below the 200 day moving average, and then what was a strangely symmetrical mirror image signal, a June gap to the upside just below the 200 day line. Of course, these two signals added up to a two month island bottom formation on the daily chart of Sage, meaning that we had a very solid reversal on the buy side for the middle of 2012. Indeed, the positivity was added to by a late August golden cross buy signal between the 50 day and 200 day moving averages, with a net effect of all of these signals being that one would be confident that Sage shares would be able to maintain a recovery trend. There was also enough here to mean that once they heard of rumours that the accountancy software group could be the subject of a takeover bid, they might very well believe it.

Payoff

While our friends of the FSA was keen to ensure that insider traders on takeover bids are punished as severely as possible, the truth of this bid chasing game is that for every 10 rumours of takeover targets at least nine come to nothing. This means that those wishing to make easy money have to get their information straight from the horse's mouth – friends and family of those doing the deal. But a chartist will try and find a situation such as Sage, where the combined effect of multiple bullish signals may mean that even if the bid rumours come to nothing the price action is so strong as to mean that you would or could gain as much as if there were a predator lurking.

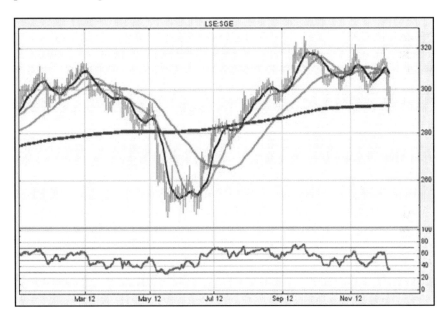

Sainsbury (SBRY): The Qataris Are Coming

The Set Up

During 2012 I read a newspaper article bemoaning the way that the Qataris have apparently already bought everything in the UK that is worth buying. Believe it or not this article was in the Daily Mail, that most patriotic of publications, which pointed out that not only had the Shard, and the Olympic village succumbed to the cheque-book of the Qataris, but that citizens of the emirate were not even bothered if their Lamborghinis get clamped outside Harrods – which is also Qatari owned. However, it would appear that one of the things which is still in a work in progress as far as our Middle Eastern friends are concerned is fully snapping up Sainsbury. In fact if you believe the Guardian in March 2012 it may be that Sainsbury avoids the clutches of Qatar, only to fall to Lebanese interest. It was said that the Miktai brothers had raised their stake to 3% in the supermarket, with their main interest in the group being as a property play.

2012 Price Action

In fact, it can be seen from the daily chart of Sainsbury that the March report of Lebanese interest in the grocer did work its magic in terms of a gap higher for the share price. Unfortunately this turned out to be a bull trap gap through the 300p level, one that contributed to the daily chart forming an island top reversal formation from March through to May. Indeed, the right side gap of this formation was through the blue 50 day moving average and provided a decent sell signal down to the June bear trap low of the year just below £2.80. Happily, from a technical analysis perspective this low of the year was not only a bear trap, but also flagged by bullish divergence in the RSI window and therefore not impossible to have got on the back of. Also worth noting is that the break back above the 200 day moving average on 29 June was a decent buy signal, something which in itself suggested the power and momentum of the recovery in the stock. The rest of the year the shares managed to accelerate within a rising trend channel, with support from extended period coming in well above the blue 50 day moving average on any dips that were seen. This is the type of price action that is only seen in the most bullish of situations.

Payoff

If you are a believer in the M&A story from the Middle East, from the second half of 2012 onwards this view was backed up by the price action and the charting configuration on the daily chart of Sainsbury. On this basis it is not a case of if but when one of the UK's leading supermarkets loses its independence.

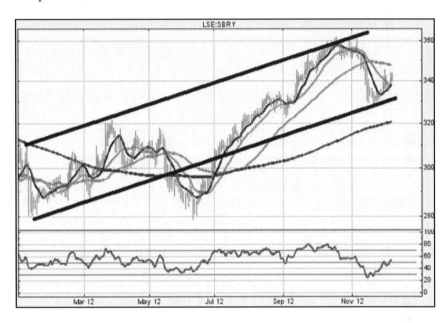

The Majors:

Sterling/Dollar: Still Made In Chelsea

The UK currency was not actually going to appear in *Lessons* this year, and in fact had there been an edition of this ebook last year or the year before, it is likely that it would not have appeared. This is because the price action of Cable has been a particularly dull market since the end of the banking sector panic in early 2009. Since then, it could be argued that our currency has essentially been pegged against the dollar, as all the action really lies versus the Euro. In fact, even against the Euro there has not exactly been a trading fest in the sense that our currency remains the lesser of most evils, rather than a proxy to an economy that anyone wishes to back in a forthright way other than buying real estate in central London. Indeed, it would be interesting to know how much influence all the hot money which has propped up the pound since the financial crisis began has had? Presumably Zone 1 London estate agents have a pretty good idea.

The lessons provided by Sterling/Dollar in 2012 are essentially those on how to cope with false signals, or deal with successful ones that have very little reward in terms of price momentum/traction. On a fundamental basis the year can be divided into three parts: the initial third in which we were in the run-up to and realisation of a double dip recession, the middle - vacuous summer festivities otherwise known as the Diamond Jubilee (which I hope made money for the UK) and the London Olympics (which I also hope made money for the UK), to the end of the year dominated by the US Presidential election/Fiscal Cliff and the run-up to the UK possibly losing its AAA credit rating/triple dip recession.

While I remember, I have two points to make on this last part of 2012. The first is hands up all the silly people who wrote or discussed the prospect of Mitt Romney winning the election, when he had even less chance than Michael Dukakis of winning, and the second is that according to the Zak Mir perspective, ironically the day the Eurozone escapes a breakup/the single currency is really saved, could be very close to the day that the UK loses its Triple A crown. Put less enigmatically, when the safe haven seekers no longer feel the need to flock to London, our PIIGS-style economy outside the M25 may be obvious even to institutions as behind the curve as S&P/Moody's/Fitch.

The technical analysis highlights in 2012, if they can be called that, came from golden and dead moving average crosses between the 50 day and 200 day lines for Sterling Dollar during July on the downside (just) and September on the upside. Both were effectively leading you up the garden path in terms of selling near the bottom and buying at the top respectively. In fact, it is normally the case that the big winner trade set ups in terms of technical signals on this cross come from the dreaded bull and bear traps. These were everywhere in 2012, with for instance the July turnaround being the result of a double bear trap from below June support and leading to an eventual rally from just under $1.54 to the $1.6309 high of September.

As the year ended it was possible to get excited about Sterling on the basis of the 200 day moving average rebound in mid-November, but really one would prefer to get involved in this cross again in a big way only if there was a sustained break of $1.63. Otherwise this really looks like random price action either side of $1.60 which really doesn't suit the daily chart time frame.

Once against this year we were treated to the schadenfreude of not being a fully attached member of the Eurozone even though we pay top dollar for this privilege, a point underlined in the recent EU budget discussions. Indeed, it can be said that if anything the best thing about Sterling/Dollar is the stability we have seen relative to many other currencies, with the implication that this makes life for those attempting to do business with our transatlantic partners all the more convenient. It would also mean that if the leading US companies actually paid any tax here, they would not need to be unnecessarily concerned about adverse currency movements against them.

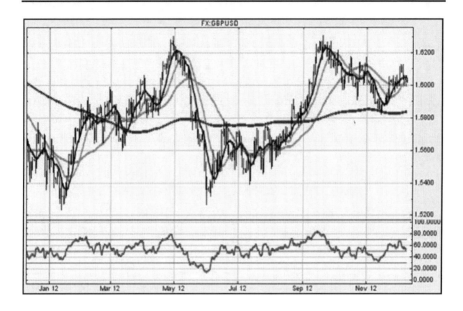

Commodities:

Gold: Still Waiting

Although the prediction game is one which is compelling, addictive, and potentially can put you on the path to untold wealth, most of the time the greatest reward here is that you end up without a pie in the face. Making predictions in the public arena is of course even more fraught in the sense that people who follow your advice can end up with a serious hole in their bank balance the existence of which can be blamed on you. This is even if it is accepted that right or wrong calling the market is done in good faith.

But from my perspective there is another twist to this game. How you react when a call is correct. While we are all supposed to learn from our mistakes, sometime successes can also be very educational. I'm reminded of this in terms of the call on gold from *101 Charts* which suggested that by the end of 2012 the metal could hit $,2000 an ounce. In fact as we now know, this market peaked out at $1,920 in September 2011, but the 1996 resistance line projection heading to $2,000 was correctly drawn.

The position now in terms of where this metal may be headed is certainly a rather conservative one as compared to a couple of years back, and has definitely been tempered by the way that gold stocks were disproportionately hammered by the post-September 2011 pullback. What we would say now quite gingerly at the end of 2012 is that while there is no weekly close back below the 200 day moving average area of $1,662, a retest of the $,1900 plus 2011 resistance should be on its way for the first half of 2013. In fact, I would go further than this and say that if the all-time record cannot be achieved within the first half of 2013 I would have to suggest that there is something wrong with the idea that this market will be able to deliver the kind of mega bull run so many are expecting.

Of course, you may well ask how gold could fail to deliver on the upside? Well, of course since gold has risen from under $300 an ounce any failure for the metal in the near future could only be regarded as a relative one. Indeed, we've already had over a year (within last year's range) in the wilderness in terms of the metal both peaking out under $2,000 an ounce, as well as gold stocks being decimated. At this stage, it would appear that given the amount of punishment that gold bugs have received in the near-term it would be safest and wisest to wait on a weekly close above the 2011 peak before even considering going long of this market again. If you are aggressive it would be $1,790 plus 2012 resistance as the entry point, but that is it.

Since the peak for gold of September 2011 it has all been about the $1,520 plus support zone for this market. This came into force twice after the all-time high was reached in 2011, with the 2012 low seen in May at $1,527 hopefully being the last such dive for this market. This is said despite the way perhaps the most simple way of describing the price action of the year-to-date is that we have been treated to a wide range between $1,520 and just under $1,800. On this basis, the way that there are no doubt plenty of damaged bulls hoping for salvation since the autumn of 2011, it may pay to wait on at least a weekly close above $1,790 from the end of 2012 before deciding that it is time to get on the bandwagon of the alleged super cycle in gold once again.

If one is kind it can be said that the price action of gold over the course of 2012 was a period of consolidation, and one that is expected to enable a continuation of the decade plus recovery in this market. However despite the bailouts, the money printing the general competitive devaluation of major currencies, it can still be said that massive upside in this metal is not yet a done deal and could be delayed far longer than many expect. Put simply, there were just too many people betting on the buy side for gold at the start of this decade, and it is not yet clear that the last of these diehards are disappearing just yet. Until they do, patience may be not so much a virtue but a necessity.

Brent Crude: Positive Consolidation

It can be said that Brent crude copied gold in 2012 in the sense that we were treated to a rather wide range, the most unusual twist being that this range was within the parameters of the previous year. While this may sound easy to negotiate, the fact that the 200 day moving average at $104 just above the middle of this on-going gyration between $90 and $115 a barrel traders were challenged in terms of the increased volatility that you normally see whether market crosses above or below the 200 day line.

Of course what we would like to know is how the consolidation/range of the last two years is going to end up? For this I have called up the weekly snapshot of Brent crude over the past six years, where can be seen how the consolidation we have been looking at over the past couple of years on the daily timeframe is a positive one above the 200 week moving average on the weekly chart. Overall the hope is that we are looking at a market in a worldwide rising trend channel from 2006 with the floor of the channel currently running level with the 200 week moving average. On this basis we would be quite confident that while $95 a barrel holds on a weekly close basis, we should see $120 barrel resistance give wagering early 2013, with a target over the next couple of years as high as $170 a barrel. While *Lessons* is ostensibly a review of last 12 months, that is not to say that there are no big calls made here as well.

Wheat: Double Trouble

As something of a footnote to the coverage of Brent crude above, it seemed almost impossible to leave the commodities zone without looking at another key market. While we have been relying on gold to act as an inflation indicator in recent years, and perhaps been somewhat disappointed at the way it has done so despite massive gains, the effect in the real world of higher inflation due to QE comes both in the form of fuel costs and food. What is interesting in the case of wheat shown here on its weekly chart is the way that going into the beginning of 2013 we appear to have a similar bull flag in place to the one seen at the end of 2006, and indicated by a black arrow. The difference between then and now is the way that the 2012 flag's price action originated in an unfilled gap to the upside. Such an unfilled gap starting a move can lead to some of the biggest spikes in price action in the financial markets. On this basis, and particularly while there is no sustained price action back below the late August $7.9 a bushel resistance, we would certainly be looking for the prospect of this market doubling price over the next year to 18 months. This is said on the basis that there will be a meeting with the top of a 2005 rising trend channel resistance line heading towards $16 a bushel. Indeed, it is interesting how the two markets, wheat and Brent crude, seem to be set on a similar path to extreme upside. Given the way that rising agricultural commodities prices were said to be an influence in the Arab spring a couple of years back, we can be fearful of how any fresh surge in food costs may pan out. If nothing else the chart of wheat reminds us that new regimes in the southern Mediterranean will have their work cut out to do any better than their non-democratic predecessors in terms of keeping the masses content.

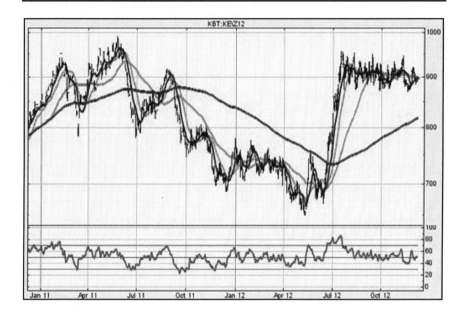

Financials:

T Bond

What an incredible market we have seen as far as the T-bond over the past 12 months has been concerned. In fact, the price action has been so regular and so simple away from the near-term noise, that it can be summed up relatively quickly in terms of the one-year snapshot. March-April saw a bear trap below the 200 day moving average, with a bounce off the floor of the main rising trend channel at $136. Then in September we saw a one touch rebound off the 200 day moving average at $145, with October witnessing a bounce off the two year rising trend channel floor at $146.17. All this adds up to a market which seems to be not only unconcerned regarding the Fiscal Cliff, but a safe haven against it. As things stood towards the end of 2012 it appeared that only sustained price action below the 200 day moving average/sub $146 can even begin to throw into doubt the prospect of a $160 plus target for early 2013. If anything, on this market one would be erring towards the upside based on the charting configuration, especially given the way that progress seems to be just about as bullish as it could be relative to the 200 day moving averages, and tests of this feature.

Indices:

FTSE 100

I suppose that it is not that easy to add value in terms of the FTSE 100 given the way that it is one of the most looked at price action traces in the country. That said, I don't think I have ever read a review of its price action on a yearly basis, or even further back. Overall, I would describe the action in 2012 as being V shaped, with this letter being formed by the classic sell in May stock market adage. It could be argued that the initial price action for the year was indeed the best, given the way that we have a surge towards the 200 day moving average then at 5,600 at the turn of the year, support established at and above it within the first couple of weeks of January and the new leg up the top of the range through 5,900 by the end of February. In fact, the key to the whole year in terms of the price action appear to be that from the December 2011 intraday low of 5,328. This came into view during May and the beginning of June, via the bear trap of that period, and I have to admit that at the time I was only looking at that W shaped price action either side of 5,300 in isolation, rather than with reference to December's previous support. This underlines the way that very often in our analysis even with the best will in the world we can to be looking at very short-term technical triggers.

In fact the big buy signal of the year came on the end of day close of 6 June at 5,384, and although it was a rocky ride back towards September's 5,900+ peak, it could be said that the signal worked well.

Following the June bear trap rebound it was the case with the FTSE 100 that despite the three steps up to steps down progression from July onwards we were treated to a rising 200 day moving average, the following month a golden cross buy signal between the 50 and 200 day moving averages, and then in September a narrow bear trap rebound back above the 200 day line. On a personal basis by the end of September I was very encouraged by the triple test of a post-July RSI support line, and feeling that the index could explode to the upside. But unfortunately reality was rather more difficult than that. In the immediate aftermath of the US Presidential Election result there was a second bear trap dip below the 200 day line then at 5,728 as an echo of the September support test. This meant that we were looking at a rather strange situation where all the bull triggers appeared to be in place, but without the market in question being able to make a break out to the upside. But of course, that is the FTSE 100 for you, frustrating until the end. As things stand just going into publication, it can be said unhelpfully that while you would not want to rule out the prospect of a decent year end rally through 6,000 after the 19 November bear trap rebound back above the September 5,634 low, such a scenario is by no means a done deal even though all the dirty work has been done by the bulls over the autumn.

What this market really needs, and has needed for years is sustained price action through 6,000 – something to call time finally on the post-dot-com bubble consolidation, and it beggars belief that over ten years after this event it just ain't happening. The message here is that it would certainly be best to wait on an unequivocal signal, a new low above 6,000, than play the antics of autumn 2012 with all the fakeouts and bear traps. At least the trend channel drawn for the FTSE 100 based at the November intraday low does have its logical target through 6,100 for early 2013.

Those looking for a sticking the neck out target would have to refer to the weekly chart I have included where the FTSE 100 based on November 2012 support has its upper parallel resistance line from 2009 heading for 7000. This I like because it ties in with Ben Gill's March 2012 call that the FTSE 100 could hit 7000 if the Bank of England, now soon to be the Bank of Canada after Mervyn King goes, continues with QE. In fact, while to suggest that 7000 will be the year end target for the FTSE 100 in 2013 is perhaps too rash for me to do, I would actually say that given the technical set up of the weekly chart, if this market cannot hit 7000 in 12 months time, we really are in the kind of "endless" Nikkei 225 nightmare we should all fear.

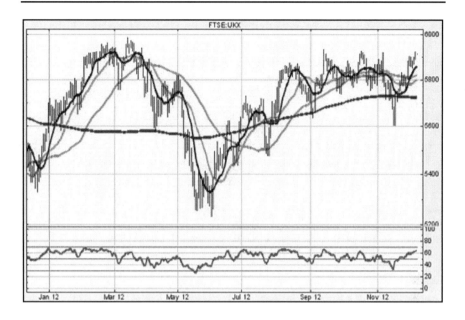

Dow

The big rally for the Dow Jones in the first half of the 2012 action stemmed from a November bear trap below the former October intraday low of 11,296. At the time it appeared that this market had turned on a dime, and perhaps it wouldn't actually be anything more than a typical end of year spent on the upside for Christmas 2011. However this idea had to be changed relatively quickly given the way that the start of January 2012 was a golden cross buy signal between the 50 day and 200 day moving averages. In some ways, the technical analysis point of view could argue that it is almost impossible for a stock or markets to start a year in any better form. Indeed, given the way that the Dow Jones behaved until the end of March you really did have a golden first quarter on your hands. The momentum here was so strong that there was no price action below the 50 day moving average between 1 January and the first week of April. This was an incredible feat and I suspect not to be repeated on many occasions this century.

The end of the line for the initial 2012 bull run came in the form of a narrow bull trap at the beginning of May above the former April peak of 12,297. But perhaps the most intriguing price action of the year came at the beginning of June where we were treated to a three-day – yes just three day – bear trap below the 200 day average. This reminds us of how important the 200 day line is, and whether or not you believe that this technical feature is merely the cause of a self-fulfilling prophecy or not, it is evident that on many occasions in the financial markets it is a key indicator. Indeed, I would go as far as to say if you were only able to use one indicator this would be it. On such a simple basis it can be said that we had a sell signal on an end of day close back below the 200 day line on 31 May at 12,393, and then a buy signal on 6 June at 12,414. So you had a small loss over these few days followed by an upside from the 6 June end of day close until September resistance of well over 1000 points. The 7 November end of day close for the Dow Jones below its 200 day moving average of 12,876 provided a similar mechanical trading opportunity.

That said, what I really liked about the post-Obama re-election Dow Jones dip as jitters regarding the Fiscal Cliff intensified was the way that the US market headed directly for a line of support from the previous December at 12500. My view is that this line will hold and that there will be a happy ending or at least a happy fudge (Eurozone like) regarding the precarious state of America's finances. At least looking at the daily chart going into the late autumn this would appear to have been the correct assumption to make. The real challenge would of course be if for whatever reason 12,500 is broken.

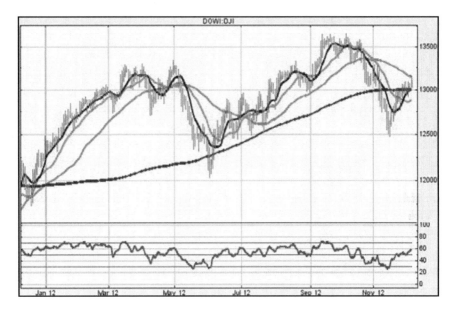

S&P

While there are obviously going to be great similarities between the price action trace of the S&P and the Dow over the course of the year, the differences are settled enough to warrant investigation. For instance the origins of the 2012 rally as far as the S&P are concerned stemmed around a bear trap rebound in December from back below the 14 December 1209 intraday floor. Unlike the Dow Jones, there was no starting gun golden cross buy signal for the S&P in 2012, instead at the end of January resist there was a normal cross between the 50 day and the 200 day lines, given that the 200 day moving average was only running flat at the time. Therefore, for the S&P it could be argued that the big buy signal here came in the form of the immediate aftermath of the May sell off. The big day in this respect was 6 June, which delivered an end of day close at 1,315, back above the black 200 day moving average then at 1275, and also well above the former May intraday low of 1291. Adding to the excitement technically speaking was the way that the 6 June daily candle came in the form of a so called Marubozo Japanese candlestick, one of the strongest buy signals around. In fact, what is interesting here is if you look at the price action of 1 June you will see that it was almost a negative Marubozo in itself (daily high is the open and daily low the close) so that we saw symmetry in terms of the speed of the downside and the bounce in recovery at the beginning of June.

Perhaps the other most noteworthy aspect of the S&P's price action in June 2012 comes in the form of what happened here at the end of August, something I underlined at the time. We can see how the late August intraday support was 1,397 while the late July peak was just under 1392. This difference between the new support and old resistance is only seen in the most bullish of situations, and certainly delivered the goods in terms of the way the S&P rallied through the start of September, fuelled by QE3 expectations. However, I would suggest that while there was a decent rally in September, this market should really have broken through 1,500 over the early autumn. Therefore the performance was somewhat disappointing relative to the set up. Indeed, it could be argued that following the September-October triple top neckline breakdown in early November on an end of day close back below 1,425, the loss of 1,392 soon after really was all the more effective as a secondary sell signal as well as being a sign that this market had caught traders out in terms of being over bullish.

Nasdaq 100

I suppose that the only signal that could be regarded as better than a golden cross between the 50 day and 200 day moving averages to start any year would be what we have seen on the Nasdaq daily chart to begin 2012. Indeed, the Nasdaq delivered an incredibly powerful-looking gap through not only the 200 day line but also the 10, 20 and 50 day moving averages. I cannot imagine that any year would start on a brighter note technically, ever. Perhaps saying this it may be argued that the price action of the leading tech stock index of the US was actually something of an anti-climax after April. But at least before April we were treated to an extreme move to the upside, a point witnessed by the way that over the three-month period the price action only dipped below the green 10 day moving average on two occasions. Weeks and weeks spent above the 10 day moving average are simply not what you normally see in most stocks or markets, and really is a sign of something special going on, or of course that you may be in the final stages of a bubble. Actually, it has to be admitted rather grudgingly that 2012 was the year when early on the financial media were questioning whether we were in the latter stages of a bubble for tech stocks, especially the social media area in the run-up to the Facebook IPO, and just for a change you could say they got it right.

What can be said as a whole in terms of the Nasdaq 2012 is that for the most part we were treated to very clear-cut signals at the major turning points. Indeed, it can be seen that the May sell off was preceded by an island top reversal signal, and just in case you missed it, this took the form of a gap up through the 50 day moving average followed by a gap down through the 50 day line. The big buy signal here came on 5 June in the form of an end of day close back above the former May 2,474 intraday low. Just in case you missed that there was a gap higher on 6 June, which gave entry point in the low 2500 zone.

Going into September the standout here in terms of the daily chart price action is the way that a pretty clear head and shoulders reversal formation was being formed, with the floor/neckline of this formation right in the middle of the early 2012 2,700-2,800 resistance zone. But just in case you missed that, 7 November's gap through the 200 day moving average then at 2,663, gave the inverse sell signal to the initial January buy gap for the US tech index. It can be said that the nightmare scenario as far as the overall pattern 2012 was concerned for the Nasdaq is that it will be a double top of trap sell signal for 2013 and beyond. Fortunately, by the end of November, with a floor of 2,494 and a still rising 200 day moving average, such a scenario was receding.

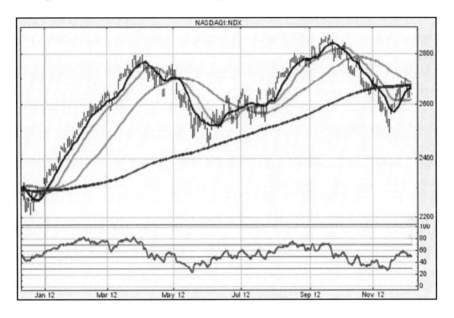

DAX

I was not actually going to include the Dax in this year's review, on the basis that I have had my Eurozone fill with the Euro/dollar, as well as the Ibex which follows. However, it would appear that the Germans are simply too important not to be given full coverage. In addition, from a technical perspective the Dax remains one of the great moving markets, and always has plenty to teach us regarding price action.

3 January delivered a gap to the upside for the Dax, a solid way to start the year, but in fact the big bull feature here during the month was the second gap on 17 January. This remained unfilled until May, underlining the way that there was power behind the upside argument to start 2012. However, it can be said that the real point of interest here in the first half of the year came in the form of the March price action on the German index, and the way that the topping out process of the month was so complex. Indeed, I would suggest that even though we were flagged to a major reversal for the Dax the double bull trap rebounds above 6,800-6,850 plus, would have made it almost impossible for the bears to gain traction. Indeed the irony is that even if you knew that this market was heading lower going into June, it would have been easier to play the index on the long side buying on dips/bear traps rather than trying to go short.

The turning point of this was in June with the pivoting either side of the 200 day moving average which at the time was trading around 6,200 mark. Something to be noted is the way that given how volatile the Dax is you will be very lucky to get in on the ground floor of any given extended move. There always appears to be final swish for the price action against you and by enough to ensure that an early entry is close to impossible. Instead, a long entry to gain advantage of the H2 2012 rally is unlikely to have been sustainable earlier than the 27 July end of day close back above the gap down from earlier that month at €6,620. It would also help by the time the floor of the rising June channel had been tested for the third time, as had the 50 day moving average for the first time as new support. Thankfully the next 600 points plus until September were delivered in a rather less rocky fashion than the June and July price action.

Finally, for the home stretch of 2012 there was the conundrum as to whether the German index would need to test the floor of the rising June channel nominally at 7,020 before continuing its recovery. The index had the problem of major 2011-2012 resistance at 7,500, and so a few steps back in order to give itself a decent run-up to the conquer 7,500 was clearly in order. While the approach of the Fiscal Cliff may have left many thinking that this was the last failure of the German index at 7,500 before an extended bear market. At least above 7,000 on weekly close basis it was valid to be looking for a long-awaited break to the upside.

IBEX

For the major markets in 2012 I have avoided trying to deliver a potted fundamental history of what happened during these 12 months, given the way that most of us will be familiar with these events and that as such I would not be adding value. Nevertheless, it may be that in the case of the Ibex/leading Spanish stocks, it would be fair to add a little background at least to the daily chart. This is because over the past few years I have been living in Pamplona, northern Spain. I had never been to this country before I met my wife ten years ago, but when I did both the feeling was that this is a wonderful country. Apart from Pamplona northwards it has a great climate and my enthusiasm a decade ago was enough to regard Spain as having the potential of a mini America. Unfortunately, this has turned out to mean that the country has the prospect of falling off its own Fiscal Cliff in 2013 and beyond, and while it had its own civil war in the 1930s as opposed to America's in the 1860s, regionalism here (Catalonia should be launching a separate sinking ship economy soon) means that the country even now still does not fully punch its weight in terms of the business world. For instance, while Spain may have many similar offerings in terms of foodstuffs, industry, tourism, the Italians are a united force on the marketing front. Of course, the French are even further ahead as far as being kings of all things Mediterranean.

But perhaps most painful of all, in the wake of the assessment credit ratings downgrades, myriad reports and articles on the levels of unemployment indebtedness, housing bubble and numerous economic ills, it would appear that there is no one in Spain ready to rebuff the accusations, deny the exaggeration, or generally highlight all the positives. I would offer to be an ambassador myself in this respect, but do actually believe that this is the role of somebody who is Spanish, and preferably a person who can also speak English and is media savvy. Perhaps with such a counter attack and without the one-way street in terms of gloom and doom in the media, money would start flowing into Spain's banks rather than out, and a floor would be found in the real estate market. As I wish to finish on a positive note here myself, I think it should be said that we should all remember what a phenomenal company retail giant Zara owning Inditex is, and how even during the past five years when the high street in many areas has been in tatters we have seen a Spanish company grow from strength to strength. A couple of other Spanish companies which I think are incredible by the way are children's toy specialist Imaginarium and shoemaker Camper

(our Catalan friends.)

All of the above has been a rather lengthy way of getting to the Ibex, but I think it has been worth it. The daily chart since the beginning of 2011 shows a descending price channel, while the price action has generally peaked at just above the still falling 200 day moving average. Clearly, the percentage trades here and expectation is that despite the post-August break back above the 200 day line the Ibex is still a work in progress for the bears, and that breaking back below the 200 day line currently at 7,466 would lead to a partial retest of the worst levels of 2012 just below 6,000. Perhaps the main, and indeed only hope here is that we shall see support retest of at or just below the former November 2011 intraday support of 7670, thus mapping out the right-hand shoulder of an inverted double head and shoulders formation made up of the April and July lows of 2012. Of course the big unknown quantity as far as this happening or not is the exact timing of any bailout for Spain. As things stand at the moment it looks as though this particular can has been kicked down the road as far as early 2013 or perhaps even longer given the way that Spanish bond auctions for 2012 delivered the government all that it required. Indeed, it may be that if there is a rebound for the Ibex from the mid-7,000s zone, this stems from the realisation that a bailout will not be required (or be less than €50bn), rather than one being on its way relatively quickly.

Nikkei 225

I think it can be said quite fairly that sometime between the writing of *101 Charts* in December 2010 and the autumn of 2012, the idea that Western economies could be following the Japanese model of an extended decades long slow death became mainstream. However, this realisation has not yet matured into the idea that QE is a bad thing not a good thing, and should never have been deployed in the first place.

We can see how the Nikkei, like its Western counterparts at the start of 2012, delivered a tasty bull opportunity. Indeed, we were treated to a near vertical rise from 8,400 to 10,000+. However, the problem for the second half of the year has been that while the Japanese index is thankfully not heading down through a falling price channel, the range that has been in place since the beginning of June has its peak at less than half the width of the overall 2012. This implied, at least until the end of November that we are biased to the downside. But towards the end of November we had been treated to both a gap through the 200 day moving average at just over 9081 and the former September peak of 9288. This could be explained by hopes that a change of Government would weaken the Yen via QE and boost Japanese exporters. Well, so far the magic seems to have worked in advance.

This is not a situation where I enjoyed being correct for years in terms of being a mega bear of Japanese shares, especially as it has terrible implications for Western economies in general, and that includes Spain and the UK. However, it can be taken as a charting win, and one where the message on the technical front is as strong or even stronger than anything that the economists can serve up, at least in the near-term. That said, it is to be hoped that the encouraging signs here at the end of 2012 do not turn out to be the umpteenth false dawn for the 20 year plus bear market. If you believe that intervention is usually doomed to failure, then it is difficult to be optimistic for the Nikkei.

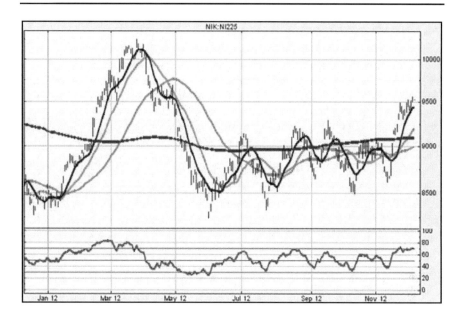

Shanghai Composite

As far as the Shanghai Composite is concerned I wanted to have some continuity with the analysis of this market delivered in *101 Charts* a couple of years back. Happily for the analysis back then and not so happily for the Chinese economy we have seen leading Chinese stocks tank, especially relative to the August 2010 resistance zone just above 3,300. To my mind with the index now around a third off the best levels of two years ago, any question of whether China has had a soft or hard landing seems rather academic. Indeed, this is academic as the situation with the FTSE 100 not being able to break its former dot-com bubble peak just below 7,000. Unless/until the UK index can break this I do not think that there is any point talking about a proper bull market being back for leading UK stocks, or indeed a recovery in the UK economy either. Clearly, not even being able to get back above 6,000 is hardly a plus point.

But getting back to the Shanghai situation, and the basic premise of the 2010 coverage was that in China we were essentially looking at Japan Mark II. I would say that this is proving to be the case even though at the beginning of November and coinciding with the 18th National Congress we were treated to a flurry of positive data on the world's second-largest economy. But of course all the worst downturns/depressions/busts have false dawns all the way down. Just like the Japanese before them, the Chinese will keep on trying to bring the good times back with infrastructure/stimulus/bailouts of one kind or another. Ironically, it is probably the case that one party state communists should be excused for not being aware that capitalism relies on the boom bust cycle and the more that you try and prevent a bust the longer that bust will last, leading to the zombielike state seen in Japan. In the UK, after the free fall of 2007-2008, we are four years into the zombie zone, so thankfully, only another 16 years plus to go. I would like to know what the odds are on when the UK will return to recession following the Q3 2012 Olympics-led dead cat bounce to the economy.

Speaking of the false dawns seen in a depression or extended bear run, it can be seen how the start of 2012 actually was a great final opportunity for leading Chinese stocks. This came off the back of a double bear trap buying opportunity that kicked in for the start of January, and was backed up by bullish divergence in the RSI window. I suppose that at that time the most obvious upside target for the index after the January turnaround was for it to hit the 200 day moving average then above 2,500, even if there was going to be a failure after that, and the multiyear bear market continues. In fact, mid-March forward saw a miss of the 200 day line, with a rather ugly bear trap below the 50 day moving average prior to the final successful test of the 200 day line in early May. This was quite a classic manoeuvre in the sense that we were treated to five consecutive days above the still falling 200 day moving average, before the market sold off sharply. Given the way that the 200 day line was falling it was almost certainly worth taking a punt on the idea that following the end of day close back below the 200 day line 2,523 on 9 May, this market would go down and stay down. Just in case you missed it the end of May/beginning of June gave an even better signal in the sense that there was a gap down through the 50 day moving average after a four-day bull trap failure below the 200 day line. As far as the final stretch of 2012 is concerned it can be seen that post-September we have been watching persistent failure coming below the 2,250 level with the likelihood being that only a weekly close back above this number would delay the prospect of at least one more test for support at the floor of a falling trend channel from December 2011's resistance line projection heading towards 2,050 in early 2013.

The great mystery of 2012 was whether China would suffer a soft or hard landing in terms of its economic growth miracle. The magic number at which things were supposed a bottom out was and still is 7% GDP growth. I simply cannot believe this will pan out as the optimists expect, if only on the basis that there has simply been too much of the credit and housing bubble in China over recent years just to simply be addressed with a few stimulus packages. But rather than merely economic guesswork, the daily chart of the Shanghai is telling us via the way that post-September 2012 resistance was below pre-December 2011 support (with the 2,250 level as the battleground) that for Chinese equities we are looking at a very bearish situation. It is inconceivable that we are on the threshold of a revival or even in a flattening out for the China economy the stock market, which is normally a leading indicator, would still be an ultra bearish mode. Indeed, if this were the case by now we would expect to see leading Chinese stocks in a rising trend channel rather than a falling one.

Dollar Index

I suppose it could be argued that the bulk of what you might say regarding the Dollar Index may be covered by analysis of say Euro/Dollar or Pound/Dollar. But looking at the daily chart of this market it can be seen that this is not really the case. What is evident though is the way that this market seems quite reliant on bull and bear traps in order to define its turning points, and ensure that even though the ranges are relatively narrow, there are plenty of the near-term trading opportunities. In fact, it may be that the pre-November period served up some of the better opportunities of the year. This is said on the basis that the double July bull trap towards 84 was the shorting opportunity of the year, while another January bull trap was also certainly playable. On the long side February and April both offered two bear trap buying chances a piece. However, long opportunity to die for was the October bear trap reversal gap fill, which combined with the way that from the beginning of November the 200 day moving average started rising, gives us at least two big plus points on the technical front. Arguably the third would be that this market managed to shake off the dead cross between the 50 day and 200 day moving averages in mid-October, something which in itself can be regarded as a substantial buy signal.

But really the main reason for including the Dollar Index here was its relevance as a proxy to Fiscal Cliff fears, as well as enabling us to try and divine what the greenback may do in 2013. From a charting perspective the price pattern here for 2012 looked to be an extended head and shoulders reversal with only sustained price action back above 81.50 really postponing a worst case scenario retest of 2011 support sub 74.

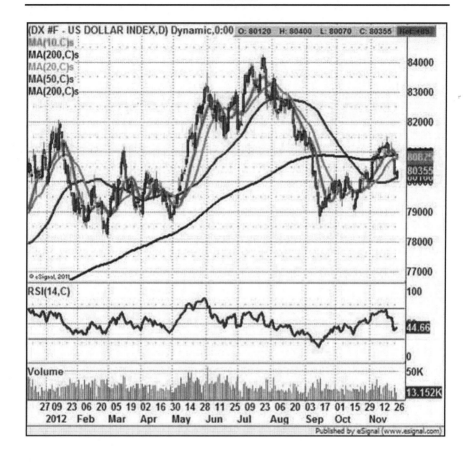

"U.S.A. Today"

Berkshire Hathaway (BRK.B): Buffett's Brilliance

The Set Up

Although *Lessons 2013* is very much a UK focused affair, and perhaps an international edition should be the focus in future, it still appears appropriate to include some of the biggest and best US companies. Certainly fitting into this category is Warren Buffett's Berkshire Hathaway. Although the man is a colossus as far as a financial markets are concerned, I do not think I chart the stock more than once a year, and this occasion appears the right time to do so in 2012.

2012 Price Action

We are in the aftermath of a double October bull trap reversal, which was accompanied by bearish divergence in the RSI window. Such combinations of signals can be regarded as particularly reliable, and of course in this case have already dragged shares of Berkshire back towards the floor of a one-year rising trend channel/200 day moving average at $83.33. This is now the likely support zone for the shares, although after such a vicious double reversal signal in October there is the risk of only temporary support coming in. Therefore, we will be keeping an eye out for any weekly close below $83.3 over the turn of the year just in case Mr Buffett's company has its share price heading for the skids. Given the way that so far support has come in well above the 200 day line it does nevertheless seem fair to give the benefit of the doubt to the upside. At least above $83 targets a notional August 2011 price channel top target of $95 for H1 2013.

Payoff

Given what a first class play this company has to be as far as the fundamental analysis brigade is concerned, charting the share price of Berkshire Hathaway is always a special event as well. The good news going into the end of 2012 is that while the shares temporarily underperformed during the autumn, they do have the plus point of being well above 200 day moving average just above $83. While this feature is held on a weekly close basis we would be recently confident that the post-June rally in the shares is set to run significantly into 2013.

Hewlett-Packard (HPQ): Too Much Autonomy

The Set Up

Hewlett-Packard is the last lesson in this ebook for 2012, just making the cut before the last week of November deadline. In fact, it could be left out as just being too late in the day as by the time the news broke regarding the information technology group crying foul over its acquisition of UK knowledge management software group Autonomy, the shaping of the book into its current form had already begun. However, there were two irresistible reasons for inclusion. The first is my hatred of printers, of which H-P is a leading culprit. Indeed, it would appear to me that mankind is able to travel to the moon and back, but so far has been unable to produce a printer which is not clunky, consumes ink like there like there is no tomorrow, has a periodic habit of either randomly printing out gibberish for no reason, and/or hitting you with a paper jam. The message is please sort this out. This is because it creates so much bad will on my part that I don't care that H-P has lost $8.8 billion due to its foolish purchase of Autonomy.

Ironically, before the deal I often joked that the share price of Autonomy was so volatile, and trading updates so badly received, largely because few in the City actually understood what the company did. It would appear that the same was true for H-P, with the added issue of there being a vacuum in its strategy after exiting the smartphone and tablet computers area. What better a plan than to buy a flash UK tech group founded by whizz kid Mike Lynch? In fact the Cambridge graduate has come under attack following H-P's accusations, of which of course being a patriotic Brit I do not believe! In fact my main issue with Mike Lynch was and is his hairstyle, which is lacking to say the least. All those millions and he could not get round to finding an appropriate follicular solution?

2012 Price Action

As far as the daily chart of Hewlett-Packard is concerned I could not resist looking at the two-year rather than the one-year view, even though ironically 2011 to 2012 was almost the same as 2012 up to 2013. This is said on the basis that both last year and this year started off with the same technical signal of a gap down through the 50 day moving average -

powerful sell signals. In addition in both years any brief spike through the 50 day line mounted to a sell point. But now in the immediate aftermath of the Autonomy charge the shock is that there was a gap down through the former November $12.36 year low, an event which suggests gathering momentum to the downside rather than some kind of selling climax. Nevertheless, we should be on guard just in case of such an implied overshoot to the downside. The beginning of the end of the nightmare could be delivered on an end of day close back above the top of the November gap down at $12.94 to suggest that we should think of putting a toe in the water in terms of bottom fishing the somewhat accident prone tech group.

Payoff

Whatever happens now it is likely that the Hewlett-Packard/Autonomy saga is likely to continue well into 2013 with mudslinging and name-calling along the way. This is exactly what I would wish to see as far as the stock market is concerned, in that as well as providing the trading platform for people to potentially make or lose millions, there is plenty of entertainment value along the way. Indeed, the $8.8bn just about makes up for all those hours of irritation over the years spent trying to print out that last page of an 11 page document just when the ink runs out, there is a paper jam, and no paper left.

Research In Motion (RIMM): Death Rattle Postponed

The Set Up

It would appear that Blackberry group Research in Motion has seen its key product get transformed from being a must have executive piece of equipment, to a brand associated with a corporate meltdown. This is certainly the case as far as the share price of RIMM has been concerned over most of 2012 despite the flying start the shares delivered back in January, along with almost everything else in the world associated with equities. But while it cannot be said that there is much to celebrate on a fundamental front in terms of any recovery prospect, at least as far as a technical concern one could say there is a light at the end of the tunnel.

2012 Price Action

As can be seen the late September low was a double bear trap reversal, the type of signal that rarely fails on the basis that the formation is designed to remove even those who correctly anticipated turnaround in a stock or market from their positions just before the change finally comes. But perhaps even better than this is the way that at the beginning of November the stock jumped to the upside leaving a one cent gap, which whether it is filled or not in the near-term underlines the way that former resistance in the $8 zone may now be coming in as new support. On this basis, particular while above the late October swing low $8.46, aggressive traders would be assuming that RIMM will at least return to the area of May resistance through $14 early in 2013. This may not be the end of the almighty bear run in this stock, although we could see a decent intermediate rally even if that is followed by an ignominious death rattle.

Payoff

The big conundrum at the end of 2012 has been whether the recovery for the share price of RIMM is indicative of the possibility that the company may survive in its current form. My pet idea is that it should team up with Nokia so the two companies can cry over how and why they lost out to Apple. But it really seems a close call as to whether RIMM will be with us this time next year, rather more close of a call than the issue of the Euro. If pushed one would imagine RIMM will see a takeover/merger, rather than continue on its present slow death trajectory.

JPMorgan (JPM): Saving The Whale

The Set Up

Being a somewhat mischievous/childish person, I really enjoyed the spectacle of London Whale being accountable for $6 billion in losses at JPMorgan, partly because it is always pleasant to watch self-important people squirm, and partly because London Whale is a first rate alias to have. Also it reminds me of the way that these days when you open up an account at any bank or broker, or ask for credit of even a trivial amount, you are asked the most personal and in-depth questions regarding your finances. But apparently the same attention to detail is missing even in late 2012 for somebody trading billions of dollars of the same financial organisation's cash. Really somebody should ensure that the same rules apply to the big people as to the little ones like you and me.

Apart from the Whale issue it was also worth noting that during 2012 JPMorgan was in the process of achieving a preliminary settlement with the SEC regarding mortgage-backed securities issues at the start of the financial crisis, now nearly five years ago.

2012 Price Action

Looking at the daily chart of JPMorgan during 2012 there are of course no prizes for guessing when the London Whale story hit the news wires. That said, it was Bloomberg who broke the story of the existence of the London Whale and his appropriately large positions on 5 April. On 13 April along with the Q1 results CEO Jamie Dimon described the whale affair as a tempest in a teapot, leading to the first wobble in the share price. What is interesting here though is the way there was an initial 1 May bull trap through $44, then a gap down through the 50 day moving average on 4 May, followed by the mega gap down on 11 May, the day after the mea culpa from Mr Dimon, whereby the tempest in a teapot was quantified as $2 billion. What was helpful here is that even late in the move and knowingly a long way down from the top in the wake of the 17 May gap to the downside one could have gone short and not have been under threat. Indeed, going into late May and early June the green 10 day moving average was an excellent trailing stop loss.

But apart from the way that there was plenty of time and opportunity to get into the JPMorgan meltdown of the spring, the real sweet spot technically must be regarded as the three day island bottom bear trap rebound in the first few sessions of June. Helping build confidence in the days following the bottom fish cue is the way that the gap up to complete the island bottom remained unfilled despite four consecutive days between 7 and 12 June in which one could see the stock willing itself to fill the gap down to $32.13. In fact, that was not all technically and in terms of the highlights regarding the recovery of JPMorgan from the Whale's financial blowhole, it was that unfilled gap above the 200 day moving average at the start of September for late comers to get on board again.

Payoff

As suggested above, JPMorgan provided great entertainment for those not involved in the stock. Shareholders were of course relying on management's attempt to spin the company out of trouble in the wake of the trading losses. The year ended with a 3 billion share buyback and an SEC deal in the pipeline so you could say that there will almost be a happy ending to the story of the London Whale.

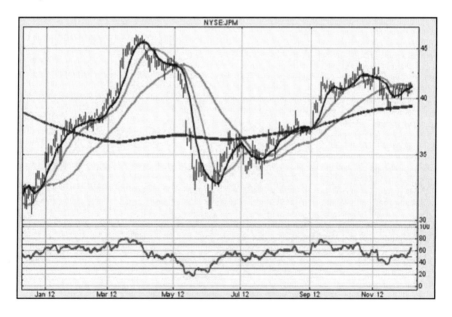

Sprint Nextel (S): Debt On Debt

The Set Up

There are a couple of major reasons why Sprint has made the grade as far as *Lessons* is concerned. The first is the way that the shares rally from $2.5 at the beginning of June to $6.04 the day before it was confirmed that Softbank was to take over the US mobile operator. The second area of interest is the way that Softbank with its $10 billion of debt was taking over Sprint with its $15 billion fiscal black hole. Perhaps, at least on this basis, the deal was a marriage made in heaven.

2012 Price Action

I am cheating a little in terms of the 2012 price action remit in the sense that for the second half of 2011 going into 2012 we have such a clear and outstanding charting setup. Arguably, the story begins with a massive gap to the downside on the daily chart of Sprint right through the black 200 day moving average at the big end of July 2011. Such moves are rarely fly by night signals, and in the case of Sprint this was enough to blow the shares back down to just $2.10 by the beginning of September from in excess of $5 at the start of the summer. In fact we can see how 2011- 2012 is a U-shaped reversal, with a first time lucky near vertical push through the 200 day moving average at the beginning of June this year. Indeed the move was so sharp that the trick here was really that one would be looking for some kind of retracement to get on board, or risk missing the boat altogether.

Payoff

As can be seen from the daily chart of Sprint over 2011-2012, those in the market seem to be counting on salvation coming from the money-losing telco for quite some time. The lesson here is that in some of the best turnaround situations for the price action as this was, you do not get a second opportunity to get on board once the momentum gets going. That said, Sprint was a classic extended reversal that both bottom fishers and the buy and hold brigade would have appreciated.

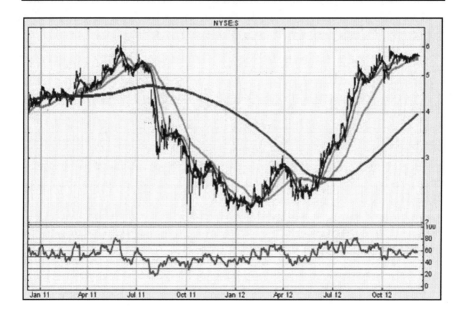

Personal Favourites: The Zak Mir 2012 Charting Gifts Collection

At the time of writing we are approaching the festive season, and after quite a tumultuous year some personal charting favourites are just what the doctor ordered in terms of providing an upbeat finale to *Lessons 2013*. A point to note is that given that this is a cheerful exercise, most of the stocks here are winners and/or are those I correctly predicted. Those which are not – mostly from the charting nightmares section – are generally the kind of charting gifts that most technical analysts would have spotted or acted upon when they presented themselves – whether bull or bear ideas. So all in all it is a happy collection that follows.

1. Leni Gas & Oil (LGO)

At least in terms of the combination of the percentage gain and the speed of the ascent it can be said that the rise and rise of Leni in the autumn of 2012 was one of the better technical tips I have made. What was so great about the set up here was the simplicity – a break of the centre of a W shaped neckline at 0.43p. On this basis it could be said that above 0.5p (a little margin of error) the target for Leni was 1p. In fact within 3 weeks the shares had nearly tripled, hitting a peak of 1.495p in the snapshot shown. From that point I was an absolute convert to the idea of single penny stocks being possible vehicles to multibagging heaven.

2. Caza Oil & Gas (CAZA)

The overall hope as far as Caza Oil & Gas was concerned going in towards the end of October is that there would be a break of the 8p to 9p resistance of an extended post-May base in for the shares to complete a new shaped reversal on the daily chart. This is essentially what was delivered by a sharp breakout end of day close on 19 October at 8.75p. The message once this was delivered is that only back below the 8p level would really be enough to delay the prospect of a retest of the early 2012 resistance through 16p. Indeed, the only surprise here is the way that the shares managed to deliver on the upside so quickly over the following few sessions. As things stand at the end of November one would be saying that while there is no end of day close back below the floor of a November gap at 14p, we will be looking for a minimum retest of the 2012 intraday peak through 22p by early 2013. The fact that there was a golden cross buy signal between the 50 and 200 day moving averages for the end of November also backed up the idea that further upside is on tap, combined as it was with a test of former 2012 resistance at 16p as new support.

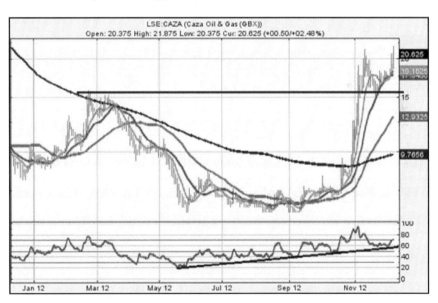

3. Sound Oil (SOU)

With Sound Oil adding to Leni (LGO) and Caza (CAZA), it can be seen how in the first three charting gifts for 2012 we essentially have the same technical structure/same sector, and a reminder of what to look out for in terms of charting prospects with the greatest upside potential. Indeed, here at Sound Oil it can be seen not only how we have a W shaped reversal with a neckline break at the beginning of October, but how this break was preceded by a narrow bear trap below the 0.4p level during September, effectively serving up a double buy signal. On this basis it was not really surprising that shares managed to more than double from the effective entry point around the 0.7p zone. In fact, there is more on the daily chart of interest here to follow in the sense that during November there was a consolidation of the sharp October spike with support coming in around the 0.95p level, a zone that ties in with the lows seen during May and June. On this basis the message was that while there was no sustained price action below 0.95p we would be looking for a minimum retest of the best levels of 2012 towards 1.6p during Q1 2013.

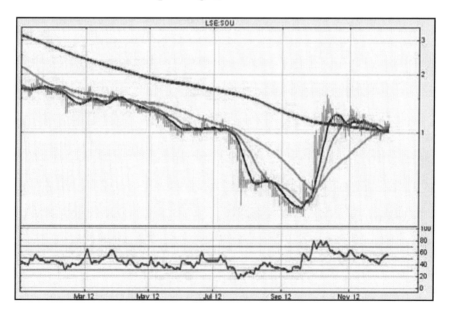

4. Ophir Energy (OPHR)

Ophir Energy works for me twice during 2012 in relatively high profile situations. The first was for the Hit List on Zaks-TA.com, the second was my maiden monthly call for Spreadbet Magazine during August/September. But perhaps the best achievement was to avoid the stock from the second week of October following the gap below the 200 day moving average. Indeed, we have been waiting for Ophir to deliver some rich old magic once again ever since, but so far those betting on the trend reasserting itself will have been hurt badly. Now, given the way that the shares are well below the day moving average near £5.30 and the aforementioned gap down from October remains unfilled, the earliest one would probably feel like getting back in the saddle on the bull tack would be after a weekly close above the 200 day moving average. Given the extended double top on the daily chart since June, it could very well be that fans of the stock may have to wait several months for the rehabilitation process to be completed.

5. Genel Energy (GENL)

While it may not actually have been the case, the impression given by former BP CEO Tony Hayward is that he was asleep at the wheel not only at the time of the Gulf disaster in 2010, but for quite long time after as well. This made it difficult to believe the charting setup on the daily chart of his new company Genel Energy from August onwards. In fact, it was a break of the former July intraday high of £6.67 on an end of day close basis on 1 August that gave the buyers the chance of a big win, if they could follow the rule of not judging a book by its cover, or on this occasion, its CEO. In fact, I was on the case a little later, looking for upside on a sustained break of the initial £7.02 intraday high of August. While it can be seen from the price action through much of August and September that there was some dithering either side of 700p, the big plus point here from a strategic perspective was the way that after 700p was broken the lowest the shares traded was £6.70 meaning that the logical stop loss just below the old £6.67 resistance would not have been hit. The expectation as of the end of November 2012 was that the saucer bottom formation here would go on to retest the former 2012 intraday high of 930p by the end of Q1.

6. Plexus Holdings (POS)

My revived love for all things on the AIM market only reinserted itself in the autumn of 2012, meaning that I missed out on many of the juicy opportunities this area of the stock market offered up during 2012 before that time. However, I did come to the party at Plexus Holdings with a decent amount of a mega rally still to come. Indeed, October's triple unfilled gap to the upside was an incredible buy signal, clearly one I have noticed that actually trumped the strength of ARM Holdings during that month. The end of day close at 182p on 19 October broke the initial high of that month at 178.5p, and in just three sessions the shares hit £2.40. The fact that initial November support came in well above £1.80 and the old £1.78 October resistance suggests that Plexus is still very much a bull play. Only well below £1.80 zone former October resistance/November support would currently diminish the prospect of at least a £2.80 2012 price channel resistance by early January.

7. Trinity Mirror (TNI)

While in some ways the daily chart of Plexus can be regarded as almost unbeatable for any larger company, if only on the basis that the price action in more highly traded companies usually tends to be more sedate, with Trinity Mirror it could be said that Plexus essentially met its match. In fact the starting gun for Trinity was the first session of August where the shares delivered an end of day close above the neckline resistance of an extended base at and below 29p. But it was the 1 August end of day close at 31p which could have given the more progressive of traders an entry point on the open following session at 35p. From then on only an end of day close back below 31p would have been enough to scare the buyers out of position and out of a possible target as high as 75p plus by October. Interestingly, those who had not got on board at the beginning of August had the chance of entering on breaks of initial September and October highs. What was interesting here is that as we went towards the end of the year, the most optimistic targets as of March 2012 at a resistance line projection of 90p was actually coming into view as a realistic prospect for say, the end of 2012.

8. TalkTalk (TALK)

One of the best technical signals that is not often talked about – literally in this case – is that of a gap through the 200 day moving average to start an extended rally. In the case of telecom services group TalkTalk it can be seen that in May we were treated not only to a gap higher through the 200 day moving average but simultaneously through the 50 day moving average as well. Of course, we will not always be looking at a stock/market from the day that there is a gap through the 200 day line to start a bull run, but given its extended nature, you will not only have plenty of time to get on board, but also be that much more confident that once you have placed the trade you will keep on winning. In fact, the last time I spotted these shares as an opportunity was 9 November around the £1.90 level, that still left plenty of upside for the £2.20 which was achieved, and the possibility of a top of 2012 price channel top as high as £2.40 by the turn of the year.

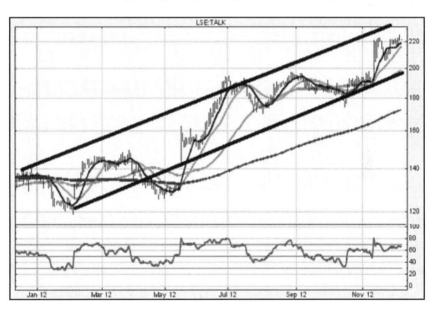

9. Dixons (DXNS)

It has to be admitted that during 2012 there were plenty of conflicting signals both on a technical and fundamental basis regarding retailer Dixons. The fact that a key member of the management left to join Apple (APPL) (leaving just months later) meant that you had be pretty sure of yourself in going long at the end of January/beginning of favourite on the multi-tested 200 day moving average rebound. That said, early in January we had been treated to a gap higher through the 50 day moving average, what can be classed as a longer term buy signal. This certainly proved to be the case in terms of what happened during the rest of 2012, although it was arguably June when the real fireworks started on the technical front. This is said on the basis that the month started off with a bear trap below the 10 day moving average which was counteracted by bullish divergence in the RSI window. It was also followed quite quickly by a gap higher through the 200 day moving average, which was by now rising, and backing up the idea of a mid-move consolidation on the early 2012 recovery to be followed by an extended leg to the upside. In fact, the expected target at the top of a rising trend channel was already achieved by early November. This meant that while some may be thinking of profit-taking, the fact that the stock found support well above former October resistance during the first part of November, meant that it was still fair to be looking for fresh gains towards as high as 30p by the turn of the year.

10. Thomas Cook (TCG)

Perhaps the most intriguing aspect of the Thomas Cook daily chart over 2012 is that rather like the Euro it was not a certainty that this stock would still alive by the end of the year. In fact, as far as the current technical perspective goes it is difficult to describe it as being in any state other than rude health. This is said on the basis of the November 2012 golden cross buy signal between the 50 day and 200 day moving averages, as well as the post-June rebound off the floor of a mildly rising trend channel from November 2011. The icing on the cake in the near-term here is the way that new support on 19 November of 5p was well above the former initial October resistance at 18.75p. Therefore, with additional backing from a rising May trendline in the RSI window, we can safely say that while there is no end of day close back below 18.75p retest of the main post-March resistance at 25p plus would appear to be on the cards for the end of 2012. Above 25p points to a swift surge to 35p early in Q1 2013.

But as well as looking forward to 2013, there is also some interest in terms of the price action in the first half of the snapshot. This is because it was an almighty swish for the shares between 10p and 30p and then back towards 13p in February. Amazingly enough by the middle of February it was possible to draw a support line and an upper parallel resistance line in the mid-20p zone, with the parallel trendlines correctly projecting the path of the stock over the following few months. In fact, the lines worked remarkably well in wake of the February peak – a touch of the 200 day moving average near 28p. Given how obedient the stock is towards these lines one would not be surprised if assuming support in the high teens does hold, 2013 eventually offers 30p plus as soon as the end of the first quarter.

11. Perform Group (PER)

From the start of the year to early July it can be said that shares in Perform Group delivered a bull run that was almost perfect in terms of having no real rocky movements. Indeed, it was the added help of an unfilled gap to the upside here in early May as well as the April to May multiple support points for the stock along the blue 50 day moving average. While it was not possible to draw the rising trend channel on the daily chart shown as is until the second half of the year, the massive distance between the share price support points and the 200 day moving average throughout the year hinted that this was a persistent uptrend contender. In fact, it is really the simplicity of the recent history of the price action as well as the multiple alignment technical signals here that go to make Perform Group one of the charting highlights of the year. For six months we have witnessed consolidation either side of the 400p level, the slow burn price action higher suggests that by the end of Q1 2013 we should be well on the way to 500p and without too much in the way of wobble. Ironically, this is one of a few situations which in you could say that the price action/setup is stable enough for you to regard the trend as your friend.

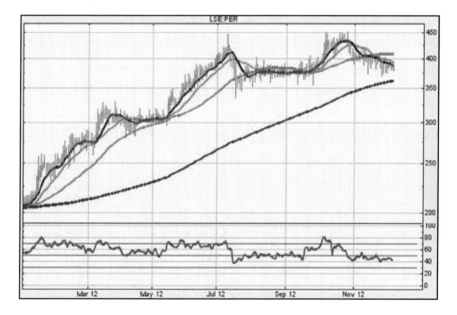

12. Cairn Energy (CNE)

It has to be admitted that shares of Cairn Energy are not normally known for playing ball in the near-term as far as short-term traders are concerned. This means that there was extra satisfaction in terms of the Zaks-TA.com portfolio being on the right side of the February gap to the upside. Indeed, that flurry on the daily chart turned out to be the best that stock achieved in terms of bullishness for the whole of 2012. Otherwise, we appeared to be looking at something of a slow death, a point underlined by the way that initial price action in May and August delivered clear bull traps, while the share price fell back accordingly. Given the uncertainties over the prospects for Cairn especially in Greenland, it may be that it will be quite a while before confidence returns to the company either on a fundamental or technical basis. Therefore, it should be said that unless the latest dip for the stock just under £2.60 proves to be start of a major turning point to the upside, we are looking at a sticky technical outlook for Cairn.

13. Bwin Party Digital Entertainment (BPTY)

I confided to the readers of Spreadbet Magazine when Bwin became one of my monthly calls there, that if a person can make a successful call in this ultra volatile and generally extremely difficult stock fundamentally and technically, that person can make a call on anything. Well, no one can get the markets right all the time, or even necessarily most of the time, but Bwin going the right way on a high profile occasion is a very pleasant experience. In fact, I would admit that suggesting a buy after the type of triple bear trap seen from August-September had only a very small chance of going wrong, especially when combined with the August uptrend line in the RSI window. In fact, although the trade was a big winner with a notional 20% exit profit in mid-October, there was an element of disappointment that the stock could not make it as high as the 200 day moving average around 127p. In fact, the way that this feature was missed even after three clear attempts in October/November could be a rather ominous sign in the months ahead.

14. BT Group (BT.A)

Increased margins due to cost-cutting as well as accelerating demand for broadband have certainly meant that over 2012 the long running battle for supremacy between BT and Vodafone has been won by the former. The reason that BT made the grade this year was off the back of cost cutting leading to improved margins and backed up by increased demand for broadband services. As far as the charting action here was concerned the main focus was between late June and early October. Indeed, the starting gun period came in the form of a gap through the 50 day moving average for whom those who bought on the open of the day after the gap higher at £2.12 were treated to a near 20p upside over the next 2 to 3 weeks. In fact it could be argued that what followed next was even more of a gift in the sense that if you follow the 23 July unfilled gap to the downside on the open of the following session at £2.19 you would have been treated to a low just under £2.02 the following day. Indeed, this dive was a buying opportunity in the sense of the day itself being a so-called abandoned baby one-day island bottom formation, as well as a bear trap intraday below the 20 day moving average at £2.05. From that point on until the shares peaked out in early September above £2.40, the stop loss on the bull argument was an end of day close back below the floor of the unfilled gap of 26 July at £2.10. All in all, this was a period of wonderful technical trading opportunities, and they were made that much more attractive by the way that BT is not usually so amenable to short-term swing trading timeframe type activities.

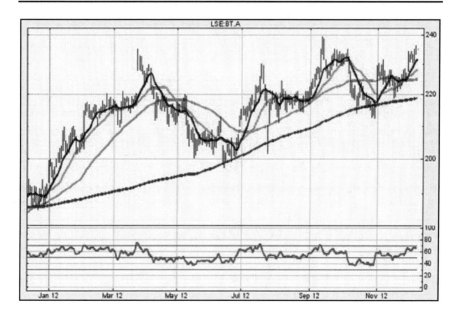

15. Scancell (SCLP)

It can be seen from the daily chart of cancer vaccine group Scancell that those searching for big penny stock winners in general, and for this one in particular, essentially had everything their own way during the course of 2012. Perhaps the best aspect of the price action over the course of this period was the way that the price action interacted with both the 50 and 200 day moving averages. This point is illustrated very well by the behaviour of this market during June when there was literally a one day dip to 7.25p and the level of the 200 day moving average at that time. For those who were watching, this was a great buy signal, as are most deflections off a rising 200 day line. In fact, moving towards the present charting position, it remains a strong sense that one would expect further progression within a rising trend channel from August. Indeed it is likely that just prior to a fresh leg to the upside we would see the share price deflect off the blue 50 day moving average currently rising at 43p. After this the stock could then go on to deliver on the promise of a final lunge to the upside which would hit the top of the three-month resistance line projection as high as 80p by the end of January at the current rate of progress.

16. GB Group (GBG)

I remember several years ago that identity management specialist GB Group (GBG) was actually one of my stocks of the year on the basis that it might do something in terms of its price action that it has been doing for the bulk of 2012. What can be seen on the daily chart of the moment is the way that there has been a rising trend channel in place since December 2011 with the floor of the channel currently level with the 50 day moving average at 90p. The view at this point is that they would expect to see further gains towards the late 2012 price channel top at £1.20 on a one to two months timeframe. If you step back and look at this chart the main point to note is that over a near two-year period there was one test of the 200 day moving average – which occurred in August last year, and that all the while since then this market has remained above or very much about the 200 day line – a state of affairs that underlines that momentum and strength behind the stock. Indeed, for the bulk of 2012 it signalled the best advice here was to actually go long of the stock on any weakness below the 50 day moving average. This remains likely to be the best policy for the first couple of months of 2013, if nothing else.

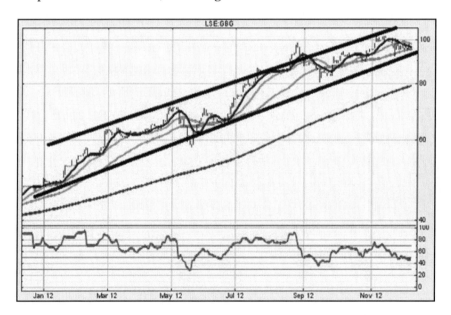

17. Pace Micro (PIC)

Clearly, given the way that shares of Pace Micro managed to rally from under 50p to over 200p during the period November 2011 to November 2012, if nothing else one can say that the shares offered plenty of excitement to those who had bought into them. Perhaps the main points to note in terms of the price action over the year was the cup and handle reversal from March through May, where the clue to future greatness came from the way that in early May support was being established at and above the blue 50 day moving average then around the 80p mark and then falling. The big giveaway as far as the most bullish situations is the way that support can be found on a falling moving average. Following this, a couple of months later was the biggest move of the year where there was a gap through the initial July intraday high of 116.75p, with the implication that time being that while there is no end of day close back below the floor to the gap at 112p we were looking for the stock to climb substantially preferably to the top of a rising May price channel at £1.60 plus. After that the name of the game for the rest the year was to hold the break of a falling red resistance line through £1.65 and attempt to target the top of the May channel as high as £2.40. As of the end of November it appeared that some of the steam had run out of the rally, but it was still the case that while there was no end of day close back below the 50 day moving average then at £1.72, one would not even blink regarding the prospects of further gains for the set-top box maker.

18. Magnolia Petroleum (MAGP)

Although it may sound strange to say it, in terms of the sheer beauty of the price action and progression higher for Magnolia Petroleum during the year, one has to say that in its own way the stock is a definite charting winner. This is over and above the fact that the stock was a 10 bagger from the lows of December last year until the November peak in 2012. Perhaps the best part of this chart is the way that from June through September there was a consolidation at and often well above the former February resistance fractionally above 2p. As I always maintain, it is a technical pillar that new support coming in at or above previous resistance is only seen in the most bullish of situations, and Magnolia proved itself to be one of them. Indeed, one disappointment in terms of the behaviour of the stock during the year, was that it could not keep the bull run extending into a new higher towards 6p, especially given the way that October support just below 4p was so much higher than the sub 3p peak seen in June. The explanation of this is that we had already seen and been treated to a couple of massive legs to the upside, and really anything greater would have been pushing it. However, this does appear to be a stop growth following for 2013 once further consolidation of the 2012 rally is delivered.

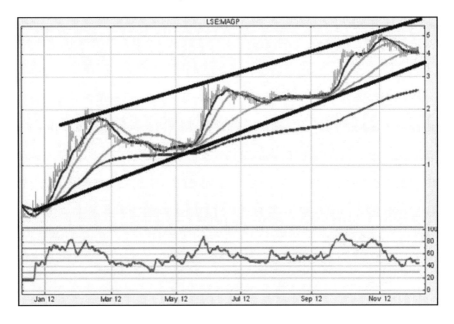

19. Barratt Developments (BDEV)

Although the March to May pullback for Barratt Developments shares would have been quite painful at the time, what was interesting here is that once the rally resumed it did so with the same super strength we witnessed from January to March. Indeed, as in the case of Magnolia Petroleum described above we were treated to persistent instances of support coming in at or above former resistance all the way from June until the beginning of November. Perhaps a message for technical traders to take home when they see such strong price action are the implications for the fundamentals. It seems obvious that if the price action is that strong then the fundamentals almost certainly will be a match to what is going on at the chart. It is also worth noting that with this kind of technical set up it can take weeks or even months for even negative newsflow to make an impact. In this instance, despite all the moaning and groaning regarding the UK housing market, or even how it is largely centred around growth in the South East and London, we would have to say that this particular market is so strong, having been boosted by foreign buying and safe haven buying over the past five years, that really would not want to bet against it for an extended period of time however bubble like the prices become. For instance, gold may have appeared to go soggy as a bull prospect over the past 12 to 15 months, but there has apparently been no such as far as the residential property market is concerned.

20. Debenhams (DEB)

Debenhams is not quite the bull Colossus that Dixons is as described above, but it did manage to double during the course of 2012. This rather makes you wonder about the real state of the UK's high street, perhaps leading us to conclude that rather than a total rout what has really happened amongst retailers is that you're either a winner or a loser, with very little in between. In other words it is very difficult just a case the long as you could perhaps when the economy was stronger. As far as the technical position of Debenhams is concerned at the moment it can be seen how there has been a rising January trendline channel dominating the scene apart from one brief period during May and June. The situation now is that the price action is some 25p above the 200 day moving average and since early June has been wholly above the 50 day moving average. The implication is that the floor of the 2012 channel at £1.07 is probably the lowest one would imagine the stock will trade prior to a meeting with the one-year resistance line projection of £1.30 over the first couple of months of next year.

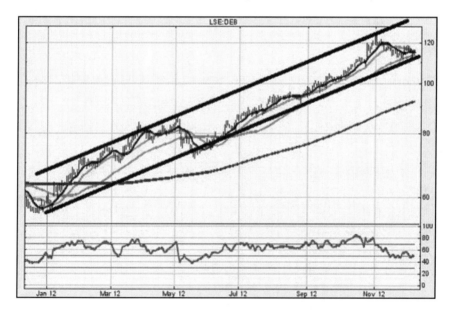

2012 Charting Nightmares Collection

Just for clarification, the charting nightmares collection refers to not only stocks that didn't behave themselves according to technical rules, or sometimes any rules. It also stands where the implication of meltdown is due to share price collapses caused by bad luck or bad management, and of course profits warnings. In fact, as we are reminded by experts both on the markets and in life in general, we learn more when things go wrong then when they go right, it could actually be that this part of the book is actually the most noteworthy.

1. Ruspetro (RPO)

Ruspetro really has been a nightmare in the sense that it represents one of the most difficult charting phenomena there are. I'm not quite sure whether this type of price action has an official name, but I'd like to call it the "back and the back". The reason for the label is because it perfectly describes what happens to traders and how they can suffer so badly in such situations. Essentially shares in Ruspetro delivered a consistent pullback from the early April peak. From a trading perspective there were many times along the way when you would have said this is it, this is the end of the retracement and we shall see the initial January to April bull run resume. Indeed, perhaps the most obvious time for recovery here was during the June-July period when the shares temporarily managed to bear trap back above the initial January support of £1.21. Indeed, there was some mileage here in the sense that late July delivered a gap through the 50 day moving average, and the shares peaked over £1.50. But the reality of this intermediate recovery was actually worse for traders in the sense that it gave them the false notion Ruspetro was back for good. Indeed, that 30p rebound may actually have been good enough to convince some in the market to ignore the gap down through the 50 day moving average – a first-rate sell signal – and then line themselves up to catch the type of falling knife move that ended up probing well below the 90p level. In fact it could be even worse in the sense that unless Ruspetro manages to recover the top of the descending April price channel/blue 50 day moving average of £1.02, there is a risk of a new leg down towards the 2012 price channel floor at 50p. What makes us fear this scenario even more is the way that post-September resistance towards £1.10 was well below the former January and June support zones near the £1.20 mark. What can be said at this stage is that for Ruspetro to be a convincing dive we would like to see not only a break of the 100p zone, we would actually like to be treated to a fresh support point above this level and even really a recovery of the initial £1.20 floor - that is how negative the set up here currently looks.

2. Aquarius Platinum (AQP)

It was an unfilled bull trap gap down on 30 January this year that effectively delivered a January island top, and was therefore a double sell signal. While the fact that the share price was well below the black 200 day moving average after multiple peaks already meant that we were looking on the negative side, after such large losses over the course of 2011 one might been thinking/hoping that an intermediate rally towards the 200p-250p zone might have have been on the cards – given the extensive losses we had already seen. This was not to be. Instead what we had were brief episodes of bear traps accompanied by bullish divergence in the RSI window such as was seen at the beginning of March and April, when there was actually money to be made, on the long side. However the same signal combination with the notional 70p plus entry would have seen buyers crushed by the end of the month below 50p. Of course, we can never expect to win on every trade and this was a notional two out of three wins in terms of the bottom fishing attempt, but for someone coming new to the Aquarius Platinum bottom fishing party during May, the experience was certainly not one to be repeated. In fact, the lesson here, as far as bottom fishing a runaway bear trend goes, is that if there is substantial space between price action peaks and the 200 day moving average driver you have to be very disciplined regarding entry points and trading stop losses or simply be a seller into strength – where the general rule is that three-day failures at the 50 day, 20 day, or 10 day moving averages normally provide for excellent near-term jobbing opportunities. That is not the end of the story of Aquarius Platinum in 2012. From August it can be seen how the stock went into a base in formation, with the message by the end of November being that after a couple of unfilled gaps to the upside through the 50 day moving average we were very much in favour of the notion that at the very least the mining stock would be able to retest September resistance at 55p - especially while the 50 day line was held.

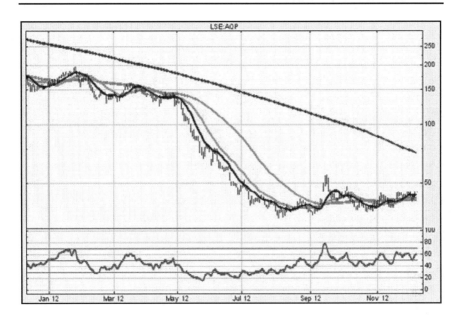

3. Talvivaara Mining (TALV)

I think it can be said quite fairly that the aftermath of the peak for gold and precious metal prices in September 2011 meant there was a period of carnage for mining stocks that to my mind would/should have been enough to put most people off the sector the rest of their lives. Just how nasty things were at the beginning of 2012 as shown by the way that Talvivaara Mining began January with an unfilled gap to the upside and two further gaps as an attempt to clear the 200 day moving average on a sustained basis. But in the end of the January peak of £3.76 was a failed gap fill of the former August 2011 gap top at £3.86 with the big sell signal being one of our favourites - a gap down through the 200 day moving average. This plunge was a great reminder that any thoughts of a trend change to the positive in this stock had to be put aside. The notional entry point after this event was on 17 February on the open of the day after the gap down at £2.89. As can be seen from that moment on short positions were rarely threatened, with this bear trend underlined by an April gap through former December support around the 200p level. Something to note here on a technical basis is the way that over and above taking a very bearish view of markets where peaks are well below the 200 day moving average, we should be looking to bull trap peaks, either below the 200 day line or gaps to the downside as offering a continuation sell message. For Talvivaara Mining these bull trap peaks were especially noticeable in June and September. Unfortunately, even by the end of November the shares having probed below 100p at worst, there is still little sign that a brave bottom fishing of the stock was indicated other than as an outright punt.

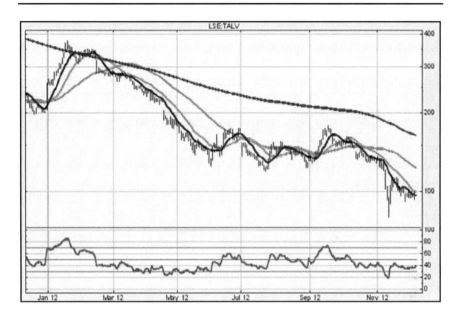

4. JJB Sports (JJB)

As far as horrible stock market experiences go it may be said that with JJB Sports, traders have the ultimate example of a pain inducing vehicle. This had everything that you do not want to experience, including white knuckle ride volatility, massive gaps, false dawn breakouts, and then all of a sudden periods of extended inactivity before the final curtain. Particularly violent was the February 2011 gap through the 200 day moving average then around 10p followed by a March support floor above the 200 day line, something which would have implied that from that moment on JJB could/should have gone up and stayed up. But of course this was not to be. The March bull trap through 35p proved to be the beginning of the end for the shares, although it was not really into the beginning of October with the loss of the 200 day moving average, and the gap down towards the end of that month that alarm bells would have started to ring. The final sadistic piece of price action came in the form of December 2011's attempted gap fill of the February move higher. This was a perfectly plausible permanent buy signal, and indeed the April break of January resistance through 15p seems to provide the backing for a sustained recovery. Once again this was the most phoney of false dawns, and a gap down through 2012 neckline support of 10p during July essentially set the seal on any hopes of JJB coming back to life. The only real positive you can take from here is that many of the signals that failed are normally relatively high probability and bankable ones. In addition, one would hope that after a couple of slaps from the stock most traders would have worked out that this was a situation best avoided. This is said on the basis that even those who correctly judged the shares to be a total short, would still have had a very rough ride over the two-year period that this charting snapshot covers.

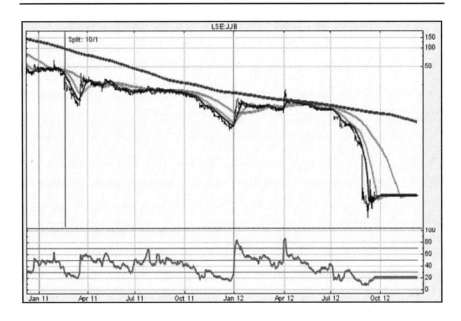

5. UK Coal (UKC)

I have already mentioned above as part of the Nightmares selection that to have a bull trap peaking out below the 200 day moving average is such a negative signal, as is a gap down unfilled through former support. And of course this is what UK Coal managed to offer us in the first three months of 2012. According to these technical rules this would have offered you a sell on the open of 15 March of 21p, with the notional trading 12p later in April. The final major sell signal here was the attempted gap fill at the start of May, but here the three-day failure to clear the 50 day moving average became a continuation sell opportunity and it was essentially downhill for the rest of the year. All the while it can be noted how there was such a relatively large distance between price action peaks and the falling 200 day moving average. Therefore on this basis one could say that shares of UK coal would appear to be heavily pressured four weeks/months going into 2013, even if there is the odd bull trap spike along the way.

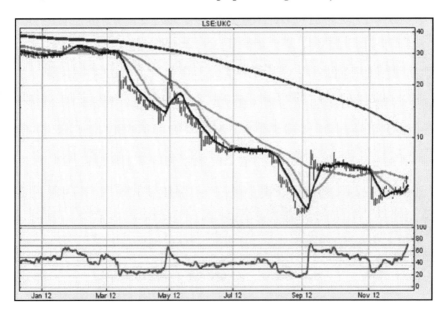

6. Falkland Oil & Gas (FOGL)

I think there is a degree of irony in terms of including Falkland Oil on the Nightmares list. This is because on the face of it the share price action over 2012 was perhaps not as bad as some of the examples already discussed. However, it can be seen that for some reason on almost all the major turning points there is a bull trap or a bear trap to start. For instance at the start of the year there was a bear trap back below former December 48p support, in March there was a bear trap below 60p stop arguably the best move of the year towards 100p, and the May peak for the stock just over 100p was also delivered as a bull trap event. I suppose it can be said that if you're waiting for bull traps or bear traps and only trade off such setups, then the price action of a stock such as Falkland Oil could be taken as a gift rather than a nightmare. Nevertheless, incredibly sharp turns and traps throughout the year as well as a crazy direction in September either side of the black 200 day moving average then around the 72p level, provide the impression that unless you really know what you are doing and are prepared to take a beating now and again, these shares are not for you. This point was underlined by the way that on the day I forwarded this ebook to the publisher Falkland Oil & Gas shares almost halved . . .

7. CPP Group (CPP)

It could perhaps be said that after the massive initial gap to the downside by CPP Group in March 2011, most sensible traders would probably have decided either to stand aside, or perhaps if they were aggressive to go short and stay short. What is a particular standout here is the way that the start of 2012 was greeted by the same type of massive gap to the downside which remained unfilled, as we saw at the beginning of the previous year. It was also noticeable that from May onwards new support struggled to come in and overlap the initially April support of 51p. But at least during October we were treated to a bear trap rebound/bullish RSI divergence, that meant at least in theory you had a chance to enter around the 10p level and see the position fly 40p plus in your favour. Of course, the setup is that it was so unbelievable I would imagine that few would have taken the opportunity.

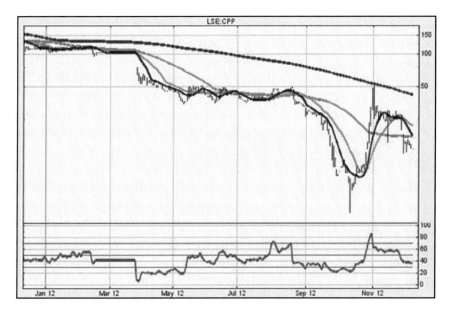

8. Chariot Oil & Gas (CHAR)

In fact, although Chariot Oil has been included in what could be described as the difficult customer section, apart from the horrific volatility over the March and September periods, charting protocol was generally obeyed. For instance, the May gap to the downside did successfully signal that the trend here had changed massively to the downside, while August's bull trap below the 200 day moving average successfully flagged a massive September gap to the downside. Admittedly, the September gap down made something of a mockery of the May-June support zone. While this may be a situation that slowly rehabilitates itself in 2013, we would really want to see something fantastic in terms of a reversal/basing signal being in place before we went for the bargain-hunting approach.

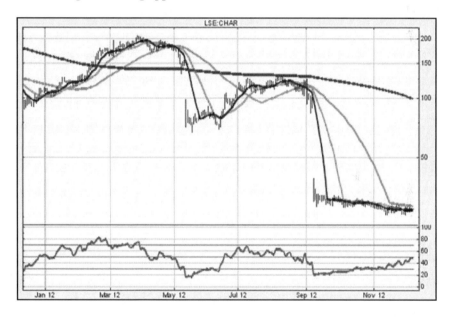

9. Lamprell (LAM)

Interestingly enough the 2011 and 2012 peaks for Lamprell before the massive gap to the downside in May were rather reminiscent of the setup in terms of the chart pattern that we saw all those years ago back at the time of the 1987 crash on the FTSE 100. But the real highlight and perhaps what can be described as agony more than anything else, was the post-May price action, as the shares attempted to find their feet. The general pattern here was of a gap down followed by a bull trap gap fill and then another gap down process which was repeated during June, July and August. That said, by the end of November there were the first signs that a selling climax had been delivered and that the 60p bear trap low on 19 November accompanied by bullish divergence in the RSI window could turn the stock around in a sustained manner. That said, during this period as little as an end of day close back below the 10 day moving average then at 75p would be enough to flush out all but the most ardent of bottom fishers, but on balance we were going with the idea that while above 75p the possibility was in place of a top of October rising trend channel target as high as 100p. This though, was definitely a situation where you are pencilling in a best case scenario more as a feelgood exercise than any real expectation of an easy ride towards that zone.

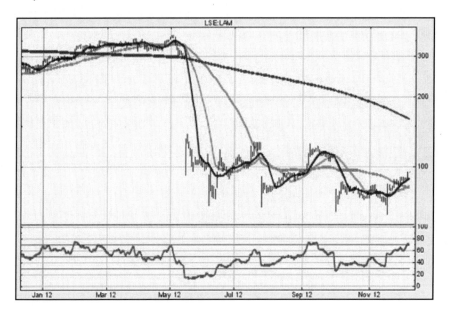

10. First Group (FGP)

Well, what a surprise, First Group, the bus and rail travel specialist was pitted against the mighty Sir Richard Branson in terms of the West Coast franchise competition, and managed to come second. One wonders what and how many strings were pulled behind-the-scenes? Presumably, many more than a typical episode of the Muppet Show? I think what can be said here from a charting perspective is the way that although the newsflow in the price action made First Group a high octane situation, most of what happened here was reasonably well flagged on the daily chart. For instance, in March we have the bull trap double top prior to the gap down, in July there was a bear trap low the former April intraday support of £1.89, and in September the following month's gap down was signalled by the gap down and gap fill just below the 200 day moving average. Therefore it can be said that while there were some very difficult situations here, undoubtedly complicated by fundamental expectations, First Group was a charting nightmare more in terms of the volatility interacting with the fast-moving fundamentals, more than anything else. At least the year appeared to be ending on a more positive/more stable note in terms of the October-November bullish divergence in the RSI window as compared to the lower November support versus October. Nevertheless, by the end of November we were waiting on at least an end of day close back above the October £1.83 intraday low, and perhaps ideally sustained price action above the 20 day moving average then at 187p, before targeting a 200p plus intermediate recovery.

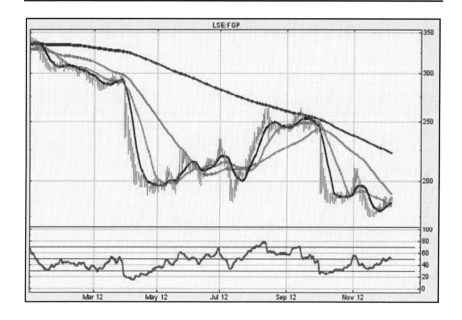

11. New World Resources (NWR)

Although it may be said that the overall price progression for New World Resources over the course of 2012 was a relatively straightforward instance of a rally until the beginning of March and then a sell off for the rest of the year, the fact that there is so much near-term noise and all in terms of the price action from day to day means that this is one of the more difficult second liners to get a handle on. Indeed, the sheer amount of the price action noise suggests that you are forced to give the shares the kind of excessive leeway that you would not normally do, just in order to ensure that any entry rate of point is based on a fair at least sensible premise. What can be said about this situation is that even when combining unrelated technical triggers share price entry and exit points remain problematic even at best. That said, a notable aspect of the post-June charting pattern is the way that most of the declines came in the aftermath of bull trap double tops that hit the bears with quite a degree of vicious price action in June/July/September and even at the beginning of November. On this basis we have a stock keen to let technical traders get the idea that rather than imposing your ideas or favourite charting setup on a particular market, it may pay to let that market essentially tell you about the signals required to best crack a sustainable trading strategy.

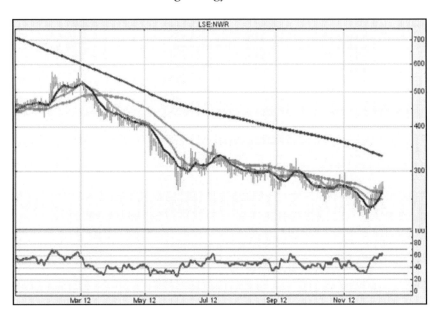

12. Rockhopper Exploration (RKH)

There are actually rather more repeats of the stocks included in *101 Charts* from two years ago than may have been expected. This is said on the basis that most minnows tend to come and go. But it must be said that both in terms of AIM stocks, in which I have now set up a Premium Blog, and many oil and gas explorers, the same names keep cropping up again and again. Rockhopper Exploration is one of the more famous plays in this respect, and I suppose judging by the price action traced during 2012, if nothing else, it is not difficult to see why the speculative interest continues. Of particular note in terms of horror one can say that the April bear trap rebound below early March £3.35 support, as well as the sharp July bull trap through former May resistance at £3.17, were both instances of the type of price action one would normally regard as being almost unplayable. At the end of 2012 we were mulling over whether the massive distance between former June support just under £2.50 and August resistance just above 200p would be enough to crush the price action on a long-term basis, or whether accompanied by bullish divergences in the RSI window we were seeing the first signs of lasting recovery? I have to admit that I was rather more biased towards the side of optimism here by the end of November, on the basis that October/November price action did consistent narrow new lows, very often the forerunner of a sustained turnaround. That said probably only a decent weekly close back above former July support at £1.65 was really going to be that big buy signal that normal traders would go for, as opposed to those who specialise in trying to catch falling knives.

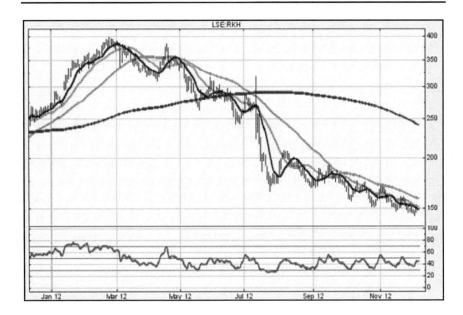

13. BG Group (BG.)

On 31 October BG Group pulled the rug from under the bulls as it cut back production guidance to flat for 2013 as supposed to the 10% rise the market been expecting. This was certainly disappointing and will have wrong footed many on the basis that going into the bolt from the blue it really did appear that the shares were building a base rather than planning a failure. Perhaps even worse it was true to say that the shares had been trading a relatively benign range between £12 and £13 since the spring, with the idea perhaps being that BG would serve up some good news to break this range to the upside, rather than the downside. Indeed this is a good example of the chart telling you everything you need to know ahead of a "surprise" event, but with those hurt the most by the price action being those that mix an element of fundamental guesswork, with the basic idea that the shares were near the bottom of the range. In fact, as we have seen in many of the Nightmare examples, the sell setup here for BG came in the form of a bull trap peak below the 200 day moving average. Indeed, the other killer blow which meant that it was very likely that a move to the downside was on its way was signalled by the 200 day line being in decline from the end of July. This is a very important point to note as it is difficult indeed for a market to snap back above a falling 200 day moving average, especially at the first time of asking. By the end of the year, the situation has stabilised to some extent, but perhaps it is fair to say that only if November bid speculation actually has any legs will those caught out by the October breakdown be sufficiently compensated. For such a scenario to pan out technically, one would really not want to see any sustained price action now back below the intraday low of 31 October at £10.50.

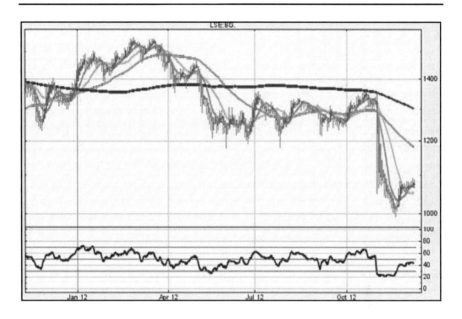

14. Man Group (EMG)

The Charting Nightmares selection that ends this e-book, was partly to include some of the year's worst meltdowns, but mostly to show that making correct technical calls on stocks and markets is not a one-way street. For instance, there is always the risk that fundamental events will intervene, and that even the very best of signals, or even a combination of signals, will simply not pan out as we want. But I have to say that in the course of compiling this top 20 horror collection, even the worst of the badly behaved stocks here have rather more logic to them now I see them alongside their peers, than they appeared to have before I started this part of *Lessons From The Financial Markets*.

In the case of Man Group, the real problems here seem to come in from the end of May when it was difficult to establish whether the shares were simply continuing the ongoing breakdown, or have finally overshot to the downside and were ready to base build. The challenge the stock delivered was that let us say in July and August there were island bottom buy patterns, with these pitted against bull trap failures below the 200 day moving average. Even with the way the stock is pivoted either side of 75p to 80p ever since it can be argued that these bull and bear signals have essentially cancelled each other out. I suppose the really smart play here would have been to stand aside after a couple of swings within the trading range. However, at the end of October it was revealed that Odey Asset Management have taken a 5% stake in the Man Group, with the reputation of the stake builder being more than strong enough to tempt smaller speculators in on the long side as well. At least as far as what can be said for the rest of the year and going into 2013 is concerned, after so many fake outs, we really would not want to see sustained price action below the former October intraday support 75p now that Odey is on board.

15. Exillon Energy (EXI)

At least until the end of July and as far as Exillon Energy is concerned, it can be said that 2012 was something of a nightmare year, especially given the way that from February to the end of July new support on the daily chart came in well below former resistance. At the same time there were a couple of turnaround signals, the first being June's bear trap rebound from below the 91p May intraday low, and the second more successful trigger being the late July bear trap below from under the initial 92.5p support of earlier that month. But perhaps the real surprise here at Exillon Energy is the way that the summer turnaround came so quickly to reverse the H1 2012 meltdown. Indeed, the turnaround was so quick, that perhaps the first chance that most traders actually had to think of getting on board alongside again was towards the end of November as the stock appeared to bounce off the floor of a rising July trend channel/black 200 day moving average at £1.39. in fact, the ideal scenario after that notional entry point was that there would be no sustained price action below the post-summer support certain of £1.30 prior to a price channel top target being hit at £1.80 over the course of Q1 2013.

16. Evraz (EVR)

I think it can be said that Evraz shares pair very well with the previous Nightmare stock of Exillon in the sense that the type of extended, turbulent base building exercise after the shares hit their lows in July, continued towards the end of the year. Indeed, the price action was too violent to be a useful trading range, and delivered several quite plausible false dawn recovery moments, most notably the way that mid-September was an island top bull trap reversal double sell signal. While it was the case that by the end of November we were enjoying a bear trap rebound from below the former October £2.26 intraday low, even at that point one would have been concerned that any future failure back below £2.26 could even be enough to trigger a fresh leg to the downside below £2.00 – largely on the basis that the difference between the price action zone and the 200 day moving average near £3.00 was still extremely significant.

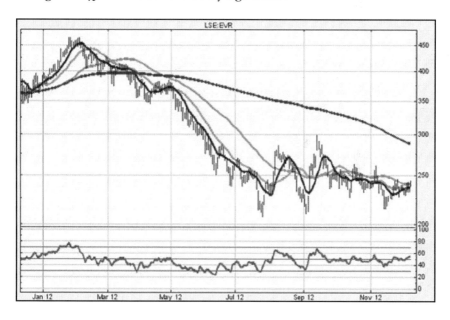

17. Centamin (CEY)

Ever since the Arab Spring began a couple of years back there was a fear associated with sentiment that summer political instability in its chosen country could lead to the kind of goalpost shifting/rug pulling fundamental event that would render it unable to carry out business in Egypt. The irony here is that its main gold mining contract at Sukari was thrown into doubt arguably just when many might have expected that the worst threat to the group's business may have been over. While it was the case that on 5 November, only a few days after the late October share price plunged, the 30-year contract was declared valid. Therefore with all this fundamental volatility It would appear that the sensible thing to do here may be to regard this issue as very much a work in progress. This is not only in the wake of increased tensions in the Middle East as a whole, but also in the wake of the new President moving to consolidate his position of power. But in the end it may actually be the chart which is telling us the most about what the prospects for Centamin actually are. This is said on the basis that after the initial shock in for the shares there was a double failure to crack the black 200 day moving average, then around the 78p level. In fact, it was our old Nightmares section favourite signal of a bull trap failure below the 200 day line that undermined the share price. Adding to the misery is the attendant break of a line of support from May at 70p. the fear at the end of November was that certainly below 70p one would regard Centamin shares as possessing a high risk of requiring a partial or even full test of the intraday year low at 35p. Even if this could be avoided, the stock would only really be regarded as an outright buy again on a decent higher low putting above the 200 day moving average, which essentially means that you are looking for sustained price action through 80p. As things stand this looks highly unlikely any time soon particularly given the way that going into towards the end of 2012 all the near-term moving average were falling quite sharply.

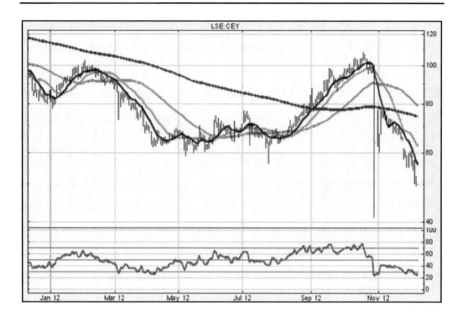

18. Cape (CIU)

I think it can be said quite fairly that commodities sector services group, Cape, has really had a year of two halves. In fact, it may be more fair to say that shareholders have experienced a happy quarter and a rather unhappy three quarters of a year in 2012. Matters reached a peak fundamental and technically in March as the group announced record revenues. However, it was noticeable even then that the higher resistance for the stock through 500p was met with bearish divergence in the RSI window. This implies that while it was initially looking positive for Cape in March on a technical perspective, the end of day close below initial March £4.25 intraday support at the end of that month, and below the 50 day moving average around 435p was flagged as the possible start of a major new bear phase. Initial May resistance at 416p – well below the former March 425p underlined the negativity, although I am sure that even the most bearish of traders were not looking for the sub 200p floor that materialised before the end of the month. What was most notable regarding the rest of the year is the way that the stock lunged from massive gaps down to partial gap fills and then gaps down again. Not exactly a smooth ride, or indeed, plain sailing for those attempting to remain one step ahead of the price action.

19. French Connection (FCCN)

French Connection is another stock that was covered in *101 Charts* a couple of years back, and it makes the grade in a negative way in 2012. Here there has been no Dixons miracle high street recovery, with most of the big action here coming in May. This consisted of an unfilled gap to the downside which not only took out May intraday support at 40p, the same day of 18 May also took out the former March intraday support at 34p. As can be seen from what happened just after that in the next few weeks, there was not even a token attempt at retracing this sharply impulsive move, with new resistance coming in well below former support going into the early summer. Indeed, the price action was so bleak for the bulk of the rest of the year that it was relatively easy to believe that the October bull trap top through the former September 26p intraday resistance - well below the falling 200 day moving average, could lead to a fresh leg to the downside either very late 2012, or in early 2013.

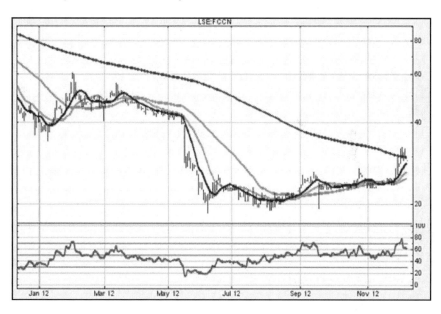

20. Kenmare Resources (KMR)

Kenmare really was something of a nightmare during 2012, with it taking several false dawn reversal signals for an enthusiast of the stock such as myself to finally refrain from pointing out bottom fishing opportunities here. Indeed, perhaps the only positive thing that can be said by the end of 2012 was that the shares have probably sickened so many it would be longs who should be on alert for a lasting reversal. That said, even though the shares are nominally at the bottom end of range of the year near 30p, the August to October head and shoulders reversal sell signal below the falling 200 day moving average means something very special will have to happen early in 2013 for this to be a bona fide bargain-hunting chance. In the meantime the best that can be said is that those who love the challenge of trying to catch a falling knife are likely to feel very much at home here at the beginning of next year.

ABOUT THE AUTHOR

Saqib "Zak" Mir was born in Glasgow, Scotland to Pakistani immigrant Doctor parents in 1966. The family moved to London in the early 1970s and Zak attended prep school and then Harrow from 1980- 1984, which was distinguished only by winning the General Knowledge Prize in 1980. Successful A Level retakes following Harrow gave him the chance to be one of the few people in the world to fail interviews for Oxford (twice), Cambridge and Harvard, although he did subsequently get the chance turn down reading Theology at Oxford. There were then a few weeks at the LSE before the international airport (the run up to the Gaddafi era) atmosphere persuaded him to enter the City. From the early 1990s Zak was a derivatives broker at various companies such as Sucden, Union Cal (later part of Man Group) and Berkeley Futures.

From 2000 the opportunities afforded by the internet and the growth of Technical Analysis led to Zak being Shares Magazine's first Technical Editor, while in the meantime providing content to now defunct dot-coms such as TheStreet.co.uk and UKInvest.com.

In 2001 Zak teamed up with Tom "Show Me The Money" Winnifrith and his T1PS.com to found Zaks-TA.com, and provides white label research to some of the City of London's largest retail brokers via Brand Communications (Branduk.net).

Zak is now a Senior Analyst at the Institute of Trading and Portfolio Management (zakmir@instutrade.com).

He is the author of several books for ADVFN, and writes for their online newspaper. He also writes for a premium blog service on ADVFN, Zak Mir's AIM Stock Charting (www.advfn.com/newsletter/zakmir/).

Zak is married with three children and lives in Pamplona, Spain.

Follow Zak on Twitter: @zakmir

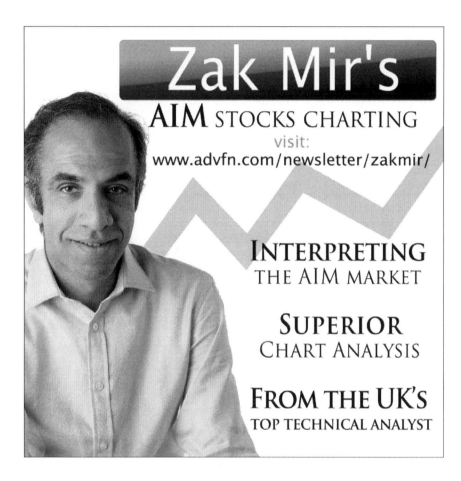

ALSO BY ZAK MIR

101 Charts for Trading Success

by Zak Mir

Using insider knowledge to reveal the tricks of the trade, Zak Mir's *101 Charts for Trading Success* explains the most complex set ups in the market. Illustrated with easy to understand charts this is the accessible, essential guide of how to read, understand and use charts to buy and sell stocks; a must for all future investment millionaires!

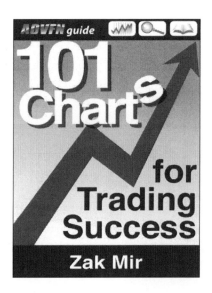

OTHER TITLES FROM ADVFN BOOKS

The Death of Wealth:
The Economic Fall of the West

by Clem Chambers

Question: What is the next economic game changer?

Answer: The Death of Wealth.

Market guru Clem Chambers dissects the global economy and the state of the financial markets and the world's economies and lays out the evidence for the Death of Wealth.

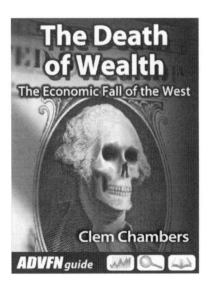

ADVFN Guide:
The Beginner's Guide to Value Investing

by Clem Chambers

The stock market is not only for rich people, or those intent on gambling. 'Value Investing' is how Warren Buffet became the richest man in the world. A method of investing in the stock market without taking crazy risks, 'Value Investing' will help you build your fortune, no matter the economic climate. Perfect for novice investors, the book clearly outlines how to choose the best stocks and how – thanks to the Internet. It is the perfect way to ensure you 'get rich slow' with minimal stress.

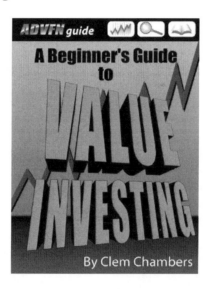

ADVFN Guide:
101 Ways to Pick Stock Market Winners

by Clem Chambers

101 tips to help day traders, investors and stock pickers to focus on what characterises a potentially successful stock. Personally researched by Clem Chambers, one of the world's leading authorities on market performance. Incisive, brutally honest and occasionally very funny, *101 Ways to Pick Stock Market Winners* is an invaluable manual for anyone wanting to make money out of the markets.

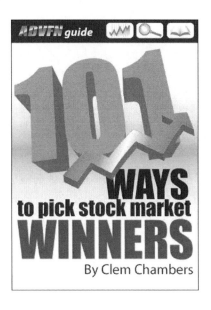

Lessons From The Trader Wizard

by Bill Cara

New from trading legend and the Free Market Patriot Bill Cara, *Lessons From The Trader Wizard* teaches the tactics and skills to beat Wall Street. Bill shows you how to navigate the new world of trading the capital markets.

Evil's Good:
Book of Boasts and Other Investments

by Simon Cawkwell

Britain's most feared bear-raider spots overvalued stocks, shorts them and goes for the kill. He's been known to make £500,000 in a single week. In *Evil's Good* – part auto-biography, part financial training guide – Simon Cawkwell tells all of his market triumphs (and downfalls) and describes the 'shorting' rules that have made him so wealthy.

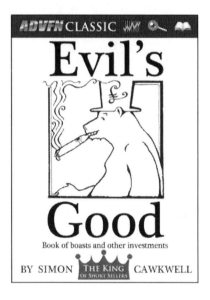

Go to www.advfnbooks.com for more information on these titles.

3594382R00106

Printed in Great Britain
by Amazon.co.uk, Ltd.,
Marston Gate.